Stock Market: Futures and Options

About the book

Dive into the world of stock market trading with "Stock Market: Futures and Options," your ultimate guide to mastering futures and options. This book breaks down complex concepts into easy-to-understand segments, starting with the fundamentals of futures and options and advancing through to sophisticated trading strategies. Learn how to use futures contracts to hedge risks and speculate on price movements, and discover how options can enhance your investment approach.

From managing risk and leveraging futures to generating income and adapting to market conditions, this guide offers practical insights and proven strategies for traders at all levels. With clear explanations, and market insights "Stock Market: Futures and Options" is your key to navigating the market with confidence and achieving your financial goals.

Author

I0477915

Table of Contents

Chapter 1: Understanding Futures Contracts

Introduction

In the world of stock markets, futures contracts are like a way to make deals today about buying or selling something at a set price in the future. This chapter will explain how these contracts work, showing how they help investors protect themselves from price changes and also how they can be used to bet on future price movements. We'll break down important details like how these contracts are set up, what's needed to participate, and how they are settled. By the end, you'll have a clear picture of how futures contracts can be a useful tool in the stock market.

Mastering Futures Contracts: A Simple Guide to Predicting and Protecting Your Investments

1) What are Futures Contracts?

Futures contracts are financial agreements to buy or sell an asset (like stocks, commodities, or currencies) at a fixed price on a set future date. Think of them as a way to lock in a price today for something you'll buy or sell later.

2) Breaking Down the Key Concepts

 (a) Contract Specifications

- Definition: These are the detailed terms of a futures contract, including the asset type, quantity, quality, delivery time, and location.

- Example: If you buy a futures contract for crude oil, the contract will specify how many barrels you're agreeing to buy, the quality of the oil, and the delivery date.

- Benefit: This standardization ensures that both parties know exactly what they're agreeing to, which reduces confusion and potential disputes.

(b) Margin Requirements

- Definition: Margin is the amount of money you need to deposit with your broker to open and maintain a futures position. It acts as a security deposit to ensure you can cover potential losses.

- Example: If the margin requirement for a futures contract is $5,000, you need to deposit this amount to secure the contract, even if the contract value is much higher.

- Benefit: Margin requirements allow traders to control larger positions with a relatively small amount of capital, amplifying both potential gains and losses.

(c) Settlement Processes

- Definition: Settlement is the process of fulfilling the terms of the futures contract. This can happen through physical delivery of the asset or through a cash settlement, where the difference between the contract price and the market price is paid.

- Example: If you hold a futures contract for gold and choose cash settlement, you'll receive the difference between the contract price and the current market price in cash.

- Benefit: Settlement processes ensure that all contracts are completed, either by actual delivery of the asset or by settling in cash, providing flexibility and liquidity.

3) Why Use Futures Contracts?

(d) Hedging Against Price Fluctuations

- Definition: Hedging involves taking a position in a futures contract to offset potential losses in another investment.
- Example: A farmer can use futures contracts to lock in a price for their crop before harvest, protecting against the risk of falling prices.
- Benefit: This provides financial stability and protects against adverse price movements, ensuring more predictable income.

(e) Speculating on Future Price Movements

- Definition: Speculating means buying or selling futures contracts to profit from expected price changes in the asset.
- Example: A trader might buy futures contracts for a stock if they believe its price will rise, hoping to sell the contracts at a higher price later.
- Benefit: Successful speculation can lead to significant profits if the price moves as anticipated, though it also involves higher risk.

(f) Leverage

- Definition: Futures contracts allow you to control a large amount of the underlying asset with a relatively small investment, thanks to margin.

- Example: With a $5,000 margin, you might control a futures contract worth $50,000.
- Benefit: Leverage can amplify gains, but also increases potential losses, making it a powerful tool for experienced traders.

(g) Liquidity

- Definition: Liquidity refers to how easily you can buy or sell a futures contract without affecting its price.
- Example: Major futures markets like oil or gold have high liquidity, allowing traders to enter and exit positions easily.
- Benefit: High liquidity ensures that you can quickly adjust your positions as needed, reducing the risk of being stuck in an unfavourable position.

4) Summary of Benefits

- Risk Management: Protects against adverse price movements in other investments.
- Profit Opportunities: Offers potential gains through speculation on price changes.
- Efficiency: Enables control of large positions with relatively small investments.
- Flexibility and Liquidity: Facilitates easy trading and adjustment of positions.
- Understanding these elements of futures contracts can help you make more informed

decisions, whether you're looking to hedge risks or capitalize on market movements.

Key Takeaways

- Futures contracts let you agree today on buying or selling an asset at a set price on a future date, helping you lock in prices and manage risk.

- They're useful for hedging against potential price changes, offering a way to protect against losses from fluctuating market values.

- Speculators use futures to bet on how prices will move, aiming to profit from future price changes without actually owning the asset.

- Key elements include understanding the specific contract details, such as the asset type, contract size, and expiry date.

- Margin requirements are essential, as they determine the initial investment needed to enter a contract and ensure you can cover potential losses.

Conclusion

Futures contracts are like financial time machines that let traders lock in prices today for transactions that will happen in the future. This chapter has taken you on a journey through how these agreements work, from their role in protecting against price swings to their potential for speculation. By mastering the basics of contract specifications, margin requirements, and settlement processes, you're not just learning about a financial tool; you're gaining a strategic asset for navigating the uncertainties of the market. As the saying goes, "The best way to predict the future is to create it," and with futures contracts, you're well-equipped to shape your financial destiny.

Chapter 2: Know What Options Are

Introduction

Welcome to the fascinating world of options trading, where strategy and opportunity intersect to create powerful investment tools. In this chapter, we'll unlock the secrets behind options contracts—financial instruments that give you the right, but not the obligation, to buy or sell an asset at a predetermined price before a set date. Imagine options as keys to potential profits or protective shields in the stock market; they can be used to amplify gains or manage risks. We'll break down the essentials of call and put options, explore their unique features, and illustrate how they can be seamlessly integrated into various investment strategies to enhance your financial toolkit.

Unlocking Options: A Simple Guide to Mastering Call and Put Contracts

A) Understanding Options Contracts

Options contracts are powerful financial tools that provide flexibility in investing. They grant you the right—but not the obligation—to buy or sell an asset at a predetermined price before a set expiration date. This flexibility can be used to hedge risk, speculate on price movements, or enhance portfolio returns.

B) Key Concepts in Options

1. Call Options

- Definition: A call option gives the holder the right to buy an asset at a specific price (the strike price) before the option expires.

- Example: Suppose you buy a call option for a stock with a strike price of $50, expiring in one month. If the stock price rises to $60, you can buy the stock at $50, potentially earning a profit of $10 per share.

- Benefit: Leverage potential gains with a relatively small investment. For instance, you might control 100 shares with a call option for a fraction of the stock price.

2. Put Options

- Definition: A put option gives the holder the right to sell an asset at a specific price before expiration.

- Example: If you buy a put option with a strike price of $40 and the stock falls to $30, you can sell it at $40, locking in a profit or minimizing a loss.

- Benefit: Provides a way to profit from or protect against declining asset prices.

C) Differences Between Calls and Puts

- Calls: Used when you expect the price of the underlying asset to rise. Ideal for bullish strategies.

- Puts: Used when you expect the price to fall. Ideal for bearish strategies.

D) Roles in Investment Strategies

- Hedging: Protect your portfolio from adverse price movements. For instance, if you hold a stock and are concerned about a decline, buying a put option can help limit potential losses.

- Speculation: Bet on future price movements without needing to buy or sell the actual asset. For example, buying call options on a stock you believe will increase in value.

- Income Generation: Write (sell) options to earn premium income. Selling call options on stocks you own can generate extra income but comes with the risk of having to sell the stock if the price rises.

E) Key Strategies for Using Options

1. Covered Call

- Description: Involves holding a long position in a stock and selling call options on the same stock.

- Benefits: Generates income from option premiums while holding the stock. Limits upside potential but provides extra cash flow.

2. Protective Put

- Description: Buying a put option while holding the underlying stock.

- Benefits: Provides downside protection. Limits potential losses if the stock price falls.

3. Straddle

- Description: Buying both a call and a put option with the same strike price and expiration date.

- Benefits: Profits from significant price movements in either direction. Useful when expecting high volatility but unsure of direction.

4. Iron Condor

- Description: A strategy involving selling an out-of-the-money call and put, while buying further out-of-the-money call and put options.

- Benefits: Profits from low volatility. Limits potential losses while earning premium income if the asset remains within a certain price range.

F) How These Strategies Benefit You

- Leverage: Options allow you to control larger amounts of an asset with a smaller upfront investment.

- Flexibility: Tailor your strategy to market conditions and personal risk tolerance.

- Risk Management: Use options to hedge against losses or protect gains.

- Income Generation: Earn premiums by selling options, enhancing portfolio returns.

Understanding and utilizing options contracts can significantly enhance your investment strategies, offering ways to manage risk and capitalize on market movements with greater precision.

Key Takeaways

- Options contracts give you the choice, not the requirement, to buy (call) or sell (put) a stock at a predetermined price before a set date.

- Call options allow you to profit if the stock price rises, while put options benefit you if the stock price falls.

- The set price for buying or selling in an option is known as the strike price.

- Options are versatile tools in investing, used for hedging risks or speculating on stock movements.

- Unlike stocks, options have expiration dates, meaning they lose value as they approach these deadlines.

Conclusion

Options contracts are versatile tools that give investors the power, but not the obligation, to buy or sell assets at predetermined prices within a set time frame. Think of them as insurance policies for your investments—calls give you the right to benefit from rising prices, while puts help safeguard against declines. As we've explored, understanding these options can enhance your investment strategy, offering both opportunities for profit and protection. By mastering the nuances of calls and puts, you unlock a world of strategic possibilities, enabling you to navigate the market with greater confidence and agility. As the old saying goes, "In investing, knowledge is power," and grasping the fundamentals of options is a key step towards achieving financial success.

Chapter 3: Learn the Basics of Futures Trading

Introduction

Welcome to the dynamic world of futures trading, where opportunities abound for both the daring and the cautious. In this chapter, we will demystify the essentials of futures trading, a realm where contracts are bought and sold with the promise to buy or sell an asset at a future date. Whether you're looking to speculate on market movements or hedge against potential risks, understanding how traders enter positions, the crucial role of delivery dates, and the strategic implications of your market predictions is key. By the end of this chapter, you'll have a clear grasp of these foundational concepts, setting you up to navigate the futures market with confidence and clarity.

Mastering Futures Trading: A Guide for Beginners

Futures trading can seem complex at first, but understanding the basics can set you on the path to becoming a savvy trader. This guide will break down the essential aspects of futures trading, offering a clear and actionable overview.

A. What Is Futures Trading?

Definition: Futures trading involves buying and selling contracts to buy or sell an asset (like commodities, currencies, or financial instruments) at a predetermined price on a specific date in the future.

Purpose:

- Speculative: Traders bet on price movements to make a profit.

- Hedging: Businesses or investors use futures to protect against price changes in the underlying asset.

Example: A farmer might sell a futures contract for corn to lock in a price and protect against the risk of falling corn prices before harvest.

B. Entering Futures Positions

How It Works:

- Buy Long: You buy a futures contract if you expect the price of the asset to rise.

- Sell Short: You sell a futures contract if you anticipate the price will fall.

Process:

1. Select the Contract: Choose a futures contract based on the asset and delivery date.

2. Deposit Margin: Pay a fraction of the contract's value as collateral.

3. Monitor the Position: Track the market to decide when to close the position.

Example: If you believe oil prices will rise, you might buy a futures contract for crude oil. If the price goes up, you can sell the contract at the higher price for a profit.

C. Understanding Delivery Dates

Significance:

- Contract Expiry: Futures contracts have a specific delivery date when the asset must be delivered or settled.
- Market Impact: Prices can be more volatile as the delivery date approaches.

Strategies:

1. Roll Over Contracts: Before the contract expires, you can buy a new contract with a later delivery date.
2. Settlement: Choose contracts that settle in cash if you do not wish to take physical delivery of the asset.

Example: If you hold a futures contract for wheat that's about to expire and you don't want to take delivery, you can roll over to a new contract with a later date.

D. Market Predictions and Position Types

Long Position:

- Objective: Benefit from rising prices.
- Strategy: Buy low, sell high.

Short Position:

- Objective: Benefit from falling prices.

- Strategy: Sell high, buy low.

Analysis:

- Technical Analysis: Use charts and indicators to predict price movements.

- Fundamental Analysis: Evaluate factors like economic reports, weather conditions, and geopolitical events that affect asset prices.

Example: If an economic report suggests a recession, you might take a short position in stocks anticipating that their prices will fall.

Key Strategies for Successful Futures Trading

- Risk Management: Use stop-loss orders to limit potential losses.

- Leverage: Be cautious with leverage, as it amplifies both gains and losses.

- Diversification: Avoid putting all your capital into a single contract or asset.

- Education: Continuously learn and stay updated on market trends and news.

Benefits:

- Mitigate Risks: Hedging can protect against adverse price movements.

- Enhance Profits: Speculation offers the potential for significant returns.

- Flexibility: Futures contracts cover a wide range of assets and time frames.

Example of Strategy Application:

Suppose you are a retailer worried about rising oil prices affecting transportation costs. You can use futures contracts to lock in current oil prices, thus stabilizing your budget and protecting against price increases.

By mastering these basics of futures trading, you'll be well on your way to navigating this exciting market with confidence. Whether you're looking to speculate or hedge, understanding these key elements will help you make informed and strategic decisions.

Key Takeaways

1. Futures Trading Overview: Futures trading involves buying and selling contracts to trade assets at a future date, enabling both speculation and risk management.

2. Entering Positions: Traders enter futures positions by agreeing to buy or sell an asset at a predetermined price and date, setting up their potential profit or loss.

3. Delivery Dates: The delivery date in a futures contract is crucial, as it determines when the asset must be exchanged, impacting the timing of your trade's settlement.

4. Market Predictions: Predictions about market movements help traders decide whether to take long (buy) or short (sell) positions, influencing their potential returns.

5. Hedging vs. Speculation: Futures can be used to hedge against price changes in assets or to speculate on market trends for potential profit, each with its own risk profile.

Conclusion

In the dynamic world of futures trading, understanding the fundamental mechanics and strategic implications is key to mastering this powerful financial tool. As we've explored, futures contracts allow traders to bet on the future price of assets, whether to capitalize on anticipated market movements or to protect against potential losses. The timing of delivery dates and the choice between long and short positions play crucial roles in this process. Just as a chess master anticipates moves ahead, successful futures traders must carefully evaluate market trends and their own predictions to navigate the complexities of this market. Remember, in the words of Warren Buffett, "Risk comes from not knowing what you're doing." By grasping the essentials of how futures trading works, you arm yourself with the knowledge to make informed decisions and potentially unlock new opportunities in your trading journey.

Chapter 4: Understand Option Pricing

Introduction

In the ever-evolving world of the stock market, understanding option pricing is crucial for anyone looking to master the art of trading. Imagine options as financial tools that give you the right, but not the obligation, to buy or sell a stock at a set price before a specified date. This chapter will demystify the pricing of these options by breaking down the key factors that influence their value—like the stock's current price, the option's strike price, the time left until the option expires, and the volatility of the market. By exploring popular option pricing models and learning how traders evaluate these factors, you'll gain a clearer picture of how options are valued and how you can use this knowledge to make more informed trading decisions.

Decoding Option Pricing

Options trading can seem complex, but understanding how options are priced is key to making informed decisions. This guide will break down the fundamentals of option pricing, helping you grasp the essential factors and strategies involved.

Understanding Option Pricing

Options pricing is influenced by several key factors, each contributing to the value of the option. Here's a detailed look at each factor:

1. Underlying Asset's Price

- **What It Is:** The current market price of the asset on which the option is based (e.g., a stock).

- **How It Affects Pricing:** The value of an option changes with the price of the underlying asset. For a call option (the right to buy), as the underlying price goes up, the option becomes more valuable. For a put option (the right to sell), as the underlying price goes down, the option gains value.

- **Example:** If you hold a call option for Company X with a strike price of $50 and the stock price rises from $50 to $55, your call option's value increases because you can buy the stock at $50 while it's worth $55.

2. Strike Price

- **What It Is:** The price at which the option holder can buy (for a call) or sell (for a put) the underlying asset.

- **How It Affects Pricing:** The relationship between the strike price and the underlying asset's price determines the option's intrinsic value. Options with strike prices closer to or below (for calls) or above (for puts) the current asset price are more valuable.

- Example: If the strike price of a call option is $50 and the underlying asset is currently priced at $50, the option has no intrinsic value but can still be valuable based on expected future price movements.

3. **Time Until Expiration**

- What It Is: The period remaining until the option expires.

- How It Affects Pricing: Options with longer times until expiration generally have higher premiums because there's more time for the underlying asset's price to move in a favourable direction. This is known as time value.

- Example: An option with six months until expiration will typically cost more than one with one month until expiration, even if all other factors are the same.

4. **Market Volatility**

- What It Is: A measure of how much the price of the underlying asset is expected to fluctuate.

- How It Affects Pricing: Higher volatility increases the potential for large price movements, which boosts the value of options. Investors are willing to pay more for the possibility of bigger price swings.

- Example: During periods of high market volatility, like during economic uncertainty, option premiums rise because the chance of significant price movements increases.

Key Pricing Models

1. Black-Scholes Model

- What It Is: A mathematical model used to calculate the theoretical price of European-style options.

- Key Factors: Uses the underlying asset price, strike price, time to expiration, risk-free interest rate, and volatility.

- Benefit: Provides a standardized method for pricing options, aiding traders in determining fair values.

2. Binomial Model

- What It Is: A model that uses a tree structure to represent possible price movements over time.

- Key Factors: Considers multiple potential future paths for the asset price, making it useful for American-style options (which can be exercised before expiration).

- Benefit: Offers flexibility to model various scenarios and exercise options at different times.

Powerful Tactics for Options Trading

1. Use the Black-Scholes Model for Fair Valuation

- Benefit: Helps in assessing whether an option is overpriced or underpriced compared to its theoretical value, guiding better trading decisions.

2. Monitor Market Volatility

- Benefit: Understanding volatility trends can help predict option price movements and adjust trading strategies accordingly.

3. Diversify Expiration Dates

- Benefit: Spreading options across different expiration dates can mitigate risk and take advantage of various market conditions.

4. Leverage the Binomial Model for Complex Strategies

- Benefit: Provides a framework for valuing options in more complex scenarios, including early exercise possibilities and varying market conditions.

5. Use Strategies Like Covered Calls or Protective Puts

- Benefit: These strategies can enhance returns and manage risk by using options in conjunction with underlying asset positions.

By mastering these elements and applying these strategies, you'll be better equipped to navigate the complexities of options trading and make more informed decisions. Understanding how options are priced is not just about knowing the numbers; it's about using that knowledge to anticipate market movements and craft strategies that align with your financial goals.

Effective Strategies for Options Trading

Understanding and employing effective strategies can significantly enhance your options trading experience. Here's a detailed look at some proven strategies, along with relevant examples to illustrate their practical applications:

1. Covered Calls

What It Is: A strategy where you hold a long position in an asset and sell call options on that same asset.

Example:

- Scenario: You own 100 shares of Company ABC, currently trading at $50 per share.

- Strategy: Sell a call option with a strike price of $55, expiring in one month.

- Outcome: If Company ABC's price stays below $55, you keep the premium from selling the call and retain your shares. If the price rises above $55, you sell your shares at $55 but still benefit from the premium received.

Benefits:

- Generates additional income from the premium received.

- Can provide a modest hedge against a decline in the asset's price.

2. Protective Puts

What It Is: A strategy where you own the underlying asset and buy a put option to protect against a potential decline in the asset's price.

Example:

- Scenario: You own 100 shares of Company XYZ, currently trading at $70 per share.

- Strategy: Buy a put option with a strike price of $65, expiring in one month.

- Outcome: If Company XYZ's price drops below $65, you can sell your shares at the $65 strike price, limiting your losses. If the price remains above $65, you let the put option expire but retain your shares and benefit from any potential price appreciation.

Benefits:

- Provides downside protection for your asset.

- Allows you to participate in any upside potential while limiting losses.

3. Bull Call Spread

What It Is: A strategy that involves buying a call option with a lower strike price and selling another call option with a higher strike price, both with the same expiration date.

Example:

- Scenario: You expect Company DEF's stock price to rise but want to limit costs.

- Strategy: Buy a call option with a strike price of $50 and sell a call option with a strike price of $55, both expiring in one month.

- Outcome: Your maximum profit is capped at $55 minus the initial cost of the spread. If Company DEF's stock price rises above $55, your profit is capped, but you benefit from the initial lower cost of entering the trade.

Benefits:

- Reduces the cost of the trade compared to buying a single call option.

- Limits both potential losses and gains, making it suitable for moderately bullish market conditions.

4. Iron Condor

What It Is: A strategy involving four options: selling an out-of-the-money call and put option, and buying a further out-of-the-money call and put option, all with the same expiration date.

Example:

- Scenario: You expect Company GHI's stock to remain stable.

- Strategy: Sell a call option with a strike price of $60 and a put option with a strike price of $50. Buy a call option with a strike price of $65 and a put option with a strike price of $45. All options expire in one month.

- Outcome: You profit if the stock price stays between $50 and $60. The maximum loss occurs if the stock price moves significantly outside these ranges, but the losses are capped by the bought options.

Benefits:

- Profits from low volatility in the underlying asset.

- Limits potential losses while allowing for a range of profit.

5. Straddles

What It Is: A strategy where you buy both a call and a put option with the same strike price and expiration date, betting on significant price movement in either direction.

Example:

- Scenario: You expect a major event to impact Company JKL's stock price but are unsure of the direction.

- Strategy: Buy a call option and a put option, both with a strike price of $75, expiring in one month.

- Outcome: You profit if the stock price moves significantly above or below $75. The strategy benefits from high volatility, but losses occur if the stock price remains close to $75.

Benefits:

- Potential for significant profit if the underlying asset makes a large move.

- Useful in situations where high volatility is expected.

6. Calendar Spread

What It Is: A strategy involving buying and selling options with the same strike price but different expiration dates.

Example:

- Scenario: You expect Company MNO's stock price to remain stable in the short term but become more volatile in the long term.

- Strategy: Sell a short-term call option with a strike price of $80 and buy a longer-term call option with the same strike price of $80.

- Outcome: You profit from the time decay of the short-term option, while the longer-term option benefits from any future price movement.

Benefits:

- Profits from the time decay of the near-term option.

- Benefits from expected changes in volatility over time.

By understanding these strategies and how they apply to various market conditions, you can better manage risk and capitalize on market opportunities. Each strategy has its own set of benefits and is suited to different market outlooks and personal risk tolerance levels.

Key Takeaways

- The price of an option is driven by the underlying asset's current price, the option's strike price, and the time remaining until the option expires.

- Higher market volatility increases the potential for large price swings, which in turn raises the value of an option.

- As an option approaches its expiration date, its value typically decreases due to the decreasing time available for it to become profitable.

- Traders use models like the Black-Scholes to estimate the fair value of options based on factors such as the asset price, strike price, volatility, and time to expiration.

- Key metrics known as "Greeks" (Delta, Gamma, Theta, Vega, and Rho) help traders understand how different factors affect an option's price and manage their trading risks effectively.

Conclusion

Understanding option pricing is like mastering the art of predicting the future with a touch of science. Just as a painter uses various colours to create a masterpiece, traders use factors such as the underlying asset's price, the strike price, time until expiration, and market volatility to value options. This chapter unveils the intricacies of option pricing models, equipping you with the tools to decode how these elements interplay to determine an option's worth. By grasping these concepts, you can navigate the complexities of the market with greater confidence, transforming uncertainty into opportunity. As the saying goes,

"Knowledge is the new currency," and in the world of options, understanding these pricing dynamics is your key to investing success.

Chapter 5: Identify Basic Futures & Options Strategies

Introduction

Welcome to the world of stock market strategies, where smart decisions can turn opportunities into profits. In this chapter, we'll dive into the basics of futures and options trading—two powerful tools that can help you navigate the market's twists and turns. Futures trading involves betting on whether prices will rise or fall, while options give you the flexibility to buy or sell stocks at predetermined prices. Whether you're aiming to capitalize on market trends or protect your investments, understanding these strategies is key. We'll break down each approach, offering clear insights on how to use them effectively, so you can confidently after thorough research make informed trading decisions and maximize your financial success.

Navigating Futures and Options: A Simple Guide to Winning Strategies

When diving into the stock market, futures and options are two powerful tools that can help investors maximize their returns. Here's a clear, detailed look at basic strategies for both, along with practical tips on how to implement them effectively.

A) Understanding Futures: Long and Short Positions

1. Long Positions: Betting on Rising Prices

- What It Is: A long position involves buying a futures contract with the expectation that the price of the underlying asset will go up.

- How It Works: If you buy a futures contract for oil at $50 per barrel, and the price rises to $60, you profit from the increase.

- Example: You purchase a futures contract for gold at $1,800 per ounce. If gold's price climbs to $1,900, you make a profit by selling the contract at the higher price.

2. Short Positions: Betting on Falling Prices

- What It Is: A short position involves selling a futures contract with the anticipation that the price of the underlying asset will fall.

- How It Works: If you sell a futures contract for wheat at $5 per bushel, and the price drops to $4, you profit from the decline.

- Example: You sell a futures contract for soybeans at $12 per bushel. If the price drops to $10, you can buy back the contract at the lower price, making a profit.

B) Benefits of Futures Strategies:

- Leverage: Futures allow you to control a large position with a relatively small investment.

- Hedging: Protect against price fluctuations in assets you own.

- Liquidity: Futures markets are typically very liquid, making it easy to enter and exit positions.

C) Understanding Options: Calls and Puts

1. Call Options: The Right to Buy

- What It Is: A call option gives you the right, but not the obligation, to buy an underlying asset at a set price (strike price) before the option expires.

- How It Works: You buy a call option for Apple stock with a strike price of $150. If Apple's stock rises to $170, you can buy it at the lower strike price and profit from the difference.

- Example: You purchase a call option for a tech company with a $100 strike price. If the stock rises to $120, you can buy at $100 and potentially sell at $120.

2. Put Options: The Right to Sell

- What It Is: A put option gives you the right, but not the obligation, to sell an underlying asset at a set price before the option expires.

- How It Works: You buy a put option for Amazon stock with a strike price of $2,000. If Amazon's stock drops to $1,800, you can sell it at the higher strike price.

- Example: You purchase a put option for a retail stock with a $50 strike price. If the stock falls to $40, you can sell at $50 and make a profit.

D) Benefits of Options Strategies:

- Flexibility: Options provide various ways to profit from different market conditions.

- Risk Management: Limited risk with defined loss potential (e.g., the premium paid).

- Income Generation: Selling options can generate additional income (e.g., writing covered calls).

E) Key Strategies for Effective Implementation

- Research and Forecasting: Use technical analysis and market research to forecast price movements for both futures and options.

- Risk Management: Set stop-loss orders and limit the size of your positions to manage risk.

- Diversification: Don't put all your money into one asset or strategy; diversify to spread risk.

- Stay Informed: Keep up with market news and economic indicators that affect asset prices.

F) Example Strategy Implementation:

- Futures: If you anticipate a rise in oil prices due to geopolitical tensions, you might take a long position in oil futures.

- Options: If you believe a company's stock will rise after a strong earnings report, you might buy call options to benefit from the potential increase.

By understanding and applying these basic strategies, you can make informed decisions and potentially enhance your investment outcomes in both futures and options markets.

Examples to illustrate short-term and long-term futures, as well as put and call options:

A) Futures Contracts

1. Short-Term Futures:

- Example: Crude Oil

    - Scenario: You believe that crude oil prices will rise in the next month due to anticipated supply disruptions.

    - Action: You buy a crude oil futures contract expiring in one month at $70 per barrel.

    - Outcome: If the price of crude oil increases to $75 per barrel before the contract expires, you can sell the contract at the higher price and profit from the $5 per barrel increase.

- Example: Wheat

    - Scenario: You expect a cold snap to affect wheat crops in the next few weeks, which could drive prices up.

    - Action: You buy a wheat futures contract expiring in two weeks at $5 per bushel.

    - Outcome: If the price of wheat rises to $5.50 per bushel due to the weather impact, you can sell the contract at the higher price, making a $0.50 per bushel profit.

2. Long-Term Futures:

- Example: Gold

- Scenario: You are bullish on gold due to long-term inflation concerns and want to lock in today's prices.

- Action: You buy a gold futures contract expiring in six months at $1,800 per ounce.

- Outcome: If the price of gold rises to $1,900 per ounce over the next six months, you sell the contract at the higher price, profiting from the $100 per ounce increase.

- Example: Soybeans

  - Scenario: You anticipate that global demand for soybeans will increase over the next year.

  - Action: You buy a soybean futures contract expiring in 12 months at $12 per bushel.

  - Outcome: If the price of soybeans rises to $14 per bushel in a year, you can sell the contract at the higher price, realizing a $2 per bushel profit.

B) Options Contracts

1. Call Options:

- Short-Term Call Option:

  - Example: Tech Stock

    - Scenario: You believe a tech company's stock will rise

significantly in the next month due to a new product launch.

- Action: You buy a call option with a strike price of $150, expiring in one month, and the stock is currently trading at $145.

- Outcome: If the stock price rises to $160, you can exercise the option to buy at $150 and potentially sell at $160, making a profit of $10 per share minus the premium paid.

- Long-Term Call Option:

  - Example: Blue-Chip Stock

    - Scenario: You expect steady growth in a blue-chip company over the next year.

    - Action: You buy a call option with a strike price of $100, expiring in one year, and the stock is currently trading at $95.

    - Outcome: If the stock price rises to $120 over the year, you can exercise the option to buy at $100 and sell at $120, making a profit of $20 per share minus the premium.

2. Put Options:

- Short-Term Put Option:

- Example: Retail Stock

  - Scenario: You believe a retail company's stock will decline in the next month due to weak earnings forecasts.

  - Action: You buy a put option with a strike price of $50, expiring in one month, and the stock is currently trading at $52.

  - Outcome: If the stock falls to $45, you can exercise the option to sell at $50 and potentially buy back at $45, making a profit of $5 per share minus the premium.

- Long-Term Put Option:

  - Example: Energy Sector Stock

    - Scenario: You anticipate a long-term decline in the energy sector due to regulatory changes.

    - Action: You buy a put option with a strike price of $80, expiring in one year, and the stock is currently trading at $85.

    - Outcome: If the stock price falls to $70 over the year, you can exercise the option to sell at $80 and buy back at $70, making a profit of $10 per share minus the premium.

C) Summary of Benefits:

- Short-Term Futures and Options: Allow you to capitalize on expected price movements over a brief period. Ideal for traders looking to exploit short-term market opportunities.

- Long-Term Futures and Options: Provide a way to benefit from expected long-term trends and can be useful for investors with a longer-term outlook. They help lock in prices and hedge against anticipated future price changes.

By understanding and applying these examples, you can better navigate futures and options markets, making informed decisions based on your market outlook and investment goals.

Key Takeaways

1. Futures Trading: Taking long positions means buying futures to profit from expected price increases, while short positions involve selling futures to benefit from anticipated declines.

2. Options Basics: Buying call options allows you to profit from price rises, whereas buying put options is a strategy for gaining from price drops.

3. Risk Management: Both futures and options require careful risk management to protect against significant losses, as they involve leveraging predictions about future market movements.

4. Market Forecasts: Success with these strategies depends heavily on accurate market forecasts and understanding of underlying assets' trends.

5. Implementation Tactics: Effective implementation of futures and options strategies involves a blend of market research, timing, and clear exit plans to maximize potential gains and minimize risks.

Conclusion

In the intricate world of stock market trading, mastering the basics is crucial for navigating the complexities of futures and options. This chapter has demystified fundamental strategies like taking long or short positions in futures, and buying calls or puts in options, laying a solid foundation for savvy investing. As the renowned investor Peter Lynch once said, "The key to making money in stocks is not to get scared out of them." By understanding these strategies and their applications, you are well-equipped to make informed decisions and manage risk with confidence. Remember, investing is not about avoiding risks entirely but about managing them wisely. It involves making well-researched, educated decisions based on market forecasts.

Chapter 6: Explore Advanced Futures Strategies

Introduction

In the dynamic world of stock trading, futures contracts offer a powerful tool for sophisticated investors looking to sharpen their strategies. This chapter delves into advanced futures strategies, exploring how techniques like hedging with multiple contracts and employing futures spreads can be leveraged to capitalize on price discrepancies and effectively manage risk. By navigating these complex methods, traders can enhance their ability to forecast market movements and protect their investments, turning volatility into opportunity and setting the stage for more informed and strategic decision-making.

Mastering Advanced Futures Strategies: Unlocking Profit and Risk Management

In the world of trading, advanced futures strategies can be game-changers. They offer ways to not only boost profits but also to manage risks more effectively. Let's dive into two sophisticated techniques: hedging with multiple contracts and utilizing futures spreads.

A) Hedging with Multiple Contracts

Hedging with multiple contracts involves using several futures contracts to manage risk and protect your investments. Here's a breakdown of how this strategy works:

1. Concept:

- Hedging means taking a position in the futures market that offsets potential losses in your primary investments.

- By using multiple contracts, you can fine-tune your hedge to cover various scenarios and protect against price volatility.

2. How It Works:

- Example: Suppose you own a large amount of crude oil stock and are worried about a price drop. You can sell multiple crude oil futures contracts to hedge against this risk.

- Adjustments: If you expect short-term volatility, you might use shorter-term contracts for quick adjustments. For long-term protection, longer-term contracts are preferable.

3. Benefits:

- Risk Management: Protects your investment from significant losses during market downturns.

- Flexibility: Allows you to adjust your hedge as market conditions change.

- Precision: Fine-tunes protection to match your specific investment needs.

4. Strategies for Effective Hedging:

- Match Contract Size: Ensure the size of your futures contracts aligns with your investment exposure.

- Diversify: Use different contracts to hedge against various risks (e.g., different commodities or market sectors).

- Monitor Regularly: Adjust your hedge as market conditions and your investment position change.

B) Utilizing Futures Spreads

Futures spreads involve simultaneously buying and selling different futures contracts to profit from the price difference between them. This technique helps manage risk and capitalize on market inefficiencies.

1. Concept:

- A futures spread consists of two positions: a long position (buy) in one contract and a short position (sell) in another related contract.

- Spreads can be classified into several types, including calendar spreads (same commodity, different delivery dates) and inter-commodity spreads (different commodities).

2. How It Works:

- Example: A trader might buy a December wheat contract and sell a September wheat contract. The goal is to profit from the price difference between the two contracts.

- Arbitrage: Exploits pricing inefficiencies between contracts that should theoretically move in sync.

3. Benefits:

- Reduced Risk: Spreads are less volatile than outright futures positions, as price movements in one contract are offset by movements in the other.

- Capital Efficiency: Requires less margin than holding a single long or short position, allowing more capital to be used elsewhere.

- Market Neutrality: Reduces exposure to market-wide movements, focusing on the relative price change between contracts.

4. Strategies for Effective Spreads:

- Choose the Right Spread: Select spreads based on your market outlook and risk tolerance.

- Monitor Correlations: Ensure the contracts involved in your spread are correlated as expected.

- Use Technical Analysis: Employ technical indicators to time entries and exits effectively.

C) Key Insights

- Hedging with Multiple Contracts:

  - Protects against price drops and market volatility.

  - Offers Flexibility in managing investment risk.

  - Requires Regular Monitoring to stay effective.

- Futures Spreads:

  - Reduces Risk through offsetting positions.

  - Provides Capital Efficiency and market neutrality.

  - Needs Precise Selection and monitoring for best results.

By mastering these advanced futures strategies, traders can enhance their ability to navigate complex markets, manage risk more effectively, and potentially boost their overall profitability.

Key Takeaways

1. Hedging with Multiple Contracts: Using several futures contracts can protect against market fluctuations and reduce overall risk by balancing potential losses with gains.

2. Futures Spreads: This strategy involves taking opposite positions in related futures contracts to profit from the price difference between them, leveraging market inefficiencies.

3. Arbitrage Opportunities: By exploiting price discrepancies between different markets or contracts, traders can lock in profits with minimal risk.

4. Risk Management: Advanced futures strategies help manage risk by diversifying positions and using sophisticated techniques to mitigate potential losses.

5. Profit from Price Movements: These strategies enable traders to capitalize on small price movements and discrepancies, enhancing potential returns in various market conditions.

Conclusion

In exploring advanced futures strategies, this chapter reveals how sophisticated techniques like hedging with multiple contracts and employing futures spreads can be powerful tools in a trader's arsenal. By understanding and implementing these strategies, traders can navigate the complex waters of the futures market with greater confidence, seizing opportunities from price discrepancies while effectively managing risk. As the adage goes, "The best defense is a good offense"—and in the realm of futures trading, a well-crafted strategy not only defends against potential losses but also positions traders to capitalize on market movements. Mastering these advanced approaches equips traders with the finesse needed to turn volatility into opportunity, ultimately transforming the uncertainty of the futures market into a landscape ripe for strategic advantage.

Chapter 7: Master Options Strategies

Introduction

Welcome to the world of advanced options strategies, where we'll unlock the secrets to mastering the stock market with precision and creativity. In this chapter, we dive into the powerful techniques of spreads, straddles, and iron condors—strategies designed not just to navigate market movements but to turn them into opportunities for income and profit. Imagine having a toolkit that allows you to capitalize on both quiet and turbulent market conditions; that's exactly what these strategies offer. We'll break down each approach step-by-step, making complex concepts clear and actionable, so you can confidently leverage these methods to enhance your trading skills and maximize returns. Whether you're aiming for steady income or looking to capitalize on market volatility, you're in the right place to take your trading game to the next level.

Key Concepts in Advanced Options Strategies

Options trading can be a powerful method for generating income and capitalizing on market volatility. Advanced strategies, such as spreads, straddles, and iron condors, offer traders sophisticated tools for managing risk and enhancing returns. In this discussion, we will delve into these strategies, providing a comprehensive guide to their application and benefits.

1. Spreads: Managing Risk and Profit Potential

What is a Spread?

- Definition: A spread involves buying and selling multiple options contracts on the same underlying asset but with different strike prices or expiration dates.

- Types of Spreads:
    - Vertical Spread: Involves buying and selling options of the same type (call or put) with different strike prices.
    - Horizontal Spread: Involves buying and selling options with the same strike price but different expiration dates.
    - Diagonal Spread: Combines vertical and horizontal spreads by differing both strike prices and expiration dates.

Benefits:

- Reduced Risk: By using spreads, you limit potential losses because the risk is capped by the difference between the strike prices.

- Defined Profit and Loss: Spreads allow you to set clear profit and loss boundaries, making it easier to plan trades.

Strategies:

- Bull Call Spread: Buy a call option at a lower strike price and sell another call option at a higher strike price. This strategy profits from a moderate increase in the underlying asset's price.

- Bear Put Spread: Buy a put option at a higher strike price and sell another put option at a lower strike price. This strategy profits from a moderate decrease in the underlying asset's price.

Example:

- Bull Call Spread: If Stock XYZ is trading at $50, you could buy a $50 call and sell a $55 call. If the stock rises to $55, your profit is capped at $5 minus the premium paid.

2. Straddles: Profiting from Market Volatility

What is a Straddle?

- Definition: A straddle involves buying a call option and a put option with the same strike price and expiration date. This strategy profits from significant movement in either direction.

Benefits:

- Profit from Volatility: Straddles benefit from large price movements regardless of direction, making them ideal for earnings reports or major news events.

- No Directional Bias: You don't need to predict the direction of the move; you only need a strong move.

Strategies:

- Long Straddle: Buy both a call and put option with the same strike price. This strategy is profitable if the stock moves significantly in either direction.

- Short Straddle: Sell both a call and put option with the same strike price. This strategy profits from minimal price movement but involves significant risk if the price moves substantially.

Example:

- Long Straddle: If Stock XYZ is trading at $50, buy a $50 call and a $50 put. If the stock moves to $60 or $40, you could make a profit.

3. Iron Condors: Income Generation with Limited Risk

What is an Iron Condor?

- Definition: An iron condor involves four options: selling an out-of-the-money call and put, and buying a further out-of-the-money call and put. This strategy profits from a stable market where the stock price remains between the inner strike prices.

Benefits:

- Limited Risk and Reward: The iron condor strategy limits both potential gains and losses. It's ideal for range-bound markets.

- Income Generation: This strategy can generate income through the collection of premiums.

Strategies:

- Iron Condor Setup:
    - Sell an at-the-money call and put (the "body").

- Buy a further out-of-the-money call and put (the "wings").

- Profit Range: The maximum profit occurs if the stock price remains between the sold strike prices. Losses occur if the price moves beyond the bought strike prices.

Example:

- Iron Condor: If Stock XYZ is trading at $50, sell a $45 put and a $55 call, and buy a $40 put and a $60 call. The maximum profit is achieved if XYZ stays between $45 and $55.

Key Strategies for Success

- Know Your Market: Use these strategies when you have a good understanding of market conditions and expected volatility.

- Manage Risk: Always have a clear plan for managing potential losses. Advanced strategies should be used with an understanding of their risks.

- Stay Informed: Regularly update your knowledge about market trends and economic indicators that might affect your trades.

By mastering these advanced options strategies, traders can enhance their ability to generate income and navigate market volatility effectively. Each strategy offers unique advantages and can be tailored to fit different market conditions and personal trading styles.

Key Takeaways

1. Spreads involve buying and selling options of the same class but different strikes or expiration dates to limit risk while aiming for profit through price differences.

2. Straddles entail buying both a call and a put option on the same asset to profit from significant price movements in either direction, ideal for anticipating high volatility.

3. Iron Condors combine two spreads to create a range-bound strategy that profits from minimal price movement by balancing potential gains and losses within a defined range.

4. Income Generation can be achieved by using these strategies to collect premiums from options while managing the risk through careful selection of strike prices and expiration dates.

5. Volatility Trading involves leveraging these strategies to capitalize on changes in market volatility, either by preparing for large price swings or by benefiting from stable conditions.

Conclusion

In mastering advanced options strategies, we've navigated the intricate landscape of spreads, straddles, and iron condors, each a powerful tool in the arsenal of seasoned traders. By understanding these techniques, you're equipped to harness market volatility and craft income streams with precision. As Warren Buffett wisely noted, "Risk comes from not knowing what you're doing," and this chapter has aimed to demystify these strategies, showing how they can transform potential risk into opportunity. Whether you seek to profit from market movements or stabilize returns, these strategies offer a roadmap to more sophisticated trading. With this knowledge, you are now poised to leverage the complexities of the options market with confidence and clarity, turning insight into advantage.

Chapter 8: Manage Risk with Futures

Introduction

In the dynamic world of futures trading, mastering risk management is not just an option—it's essential for success. As traders navigate the ups and downs of volatile markets, understanding how to effectively manage risk becomes the key to safeguarding their investments. This chapter delves into powerful strategies for controlling potential losses and protecting your capital. We will explore the strategic use of stop-loss orders and position sizing techniques that can act as your financial safety net, ensuring that you stay resilient even in the face of market turbulence. By the end of this chapter, you'll be equipped with practical tools to help you navigate futures trading with confidence and security.

Mastering Risk Management in Futures Trading

Effective risk management is essential in futures trading to safeguard your capital and navigate volatile markets. In this discussion, we will explore two key strategies: stop-loss orders and position sizing. By understanding and implementing these techniques, you can better manage risk and enhance your trading success.

1. Stop-Loss Orders: Your Safety Net

What is a Stop-Loss Order?

A stop-loss order is a tool used to limit potential losses in a trade. It automatically sells a futures contract when its price reaches a predetermined level. This helps prevent losses from escalating if the market moves against you.

In-Depth Analysis:

- Prevents Large Losses: By setting a stop-loss order, you establish a point at which your position will be closed if the market moves unfavourably. This protects your capital from significant declines.

- Emotional Discipline: Having a stop-loss order in place removes emotional decision-making. You won't have to make snap decisions during market volatility, reducing the risk of holding onto losing positions out of hope or fear.

- Automation: Stop-loss orders execute automatically, ensuring that you don't miss the opportunity to limit your loss, even if you're not monitoring the market constantly.

Key Strategies:

- Determine the Right Stop-Loss Level: Base your stop-loss on technical analysis, such as support and resistance levels or volatility indicators. For instance, placing a stop-loss just below a strong support level can help you avoid getting stopped out too early.

- Use Trailing Stops: A trailing stop-loss order adjusts automatically with the market price. If the market moves in your favour, the stop-loss level follows, locking in profits while still protecting against losses.

Example:

- If you buy a futures contract at $100, you might set a stop-loss at $95. If the market falls to $95, the stop-loss order triggers, selling your contract and limiting your loss to $5 per contract.

Benefits:

- Limiting Losses: Stop-loss orders help ensure that losses are contained within your predetermined risk tolerance.
- Reduced Stress: Knowing that a plan is in place for unfavourable movements reduces stress and allows you to trade with a clearer mind.

2. Position Sizing: The Art of Balancing Risk and Reward

What is Position Sizing?

Position sizing refers to determining the amount of capital to allocate to a single trade. It's a crucial aspect of risk management that helps ensure that no single trade can cause excessive damage to your portfolio.

In-Depth Analysis:

- Control Over Risk: By adjusting the size of your position, you control the amount of risk you're exposed to in each trade. This helps manage overall portfolio risk and avoids overexposure to any single trade.
- Preserve Capital: Proper position sizing ensures that losses are manageable and that your capital

remains protected, allowing you to stay in the game even after a series of losses.

- Risk-Reward Balance: It allows you to balance potential rewards with the risk you're willing to take. This means you can pursue higher potential returns without risking an unsustainable portion of your capital.

Key Strategies:

- Calculate Risk per Trade: Determine how much of your trading capital you're willing to risk on each trade. A common approach is to risk 1-2% of your capital per trade. For example, if your total capital is $10,000, risking 1% would mean a maximum loss of $100 per trade.

- Adjust Position Size Based on Volatility: In highly volatile markets, consider reducing your position size to account for larger price swings. Conversely, in stable markets, you might increase your position size for potentially higher gains.

Example:

- If you have $10,000 in trading capital and decide to risk 2% per trade, you would risk $200 per trade. If your stop-loss is set to limit losses to $2 per contract, you can buy up to 100 contracts ($200 risk / $2 loss per contract = 100 contracts).

Benefits:

- Mitigates Large Losses: Proper position sizing ensures that even if a trade goes against you, the impact on your overall capital is minimal.

- Enhances Longevity: By managing risk effectively, you increase your chances of long-term success and avoid the risk of blowing your account due to a few bad trades.

Summary

In futures trading, managing risk effectively is vital for long-term success. By using stop-loss orders and implementing sound position sizing strategies, you can limit potential losses, reduce emotional stress, and protect your capital. Incorporating these practices into your trading routine will help you stay resilient in volatile markets and improve your overall trading performance.

Key Insights:

- Stop-Loss Orders: Automate loss prevention, reduce emotional decision-making, and protect your capital.

- Position Sizing: Control the amount of risk per trade, preserve capital, and balance potential rewards with risk.

Implementing these strategies will help you manage risk effectively and navigate the complexities of futures trading with greater confidence.

Key Takeaways

1. Stop-Loss Orders Protect Your Capital: Setting stop-loss orders helps automatically exit a trade when prices move against you, minimizing potential losses.

2. Position Sizing Balances Risk and Reward: Properly sizing your positions based on your risk tolerance ensures that no single trade can significantly impact your overall capital.

3. Volatility Requires Extra Caution: In volatile markets, tighter stop-loss orders and smaller positions can reduce the risk of large, unexpected losses.

4. Risk Management Strategies Are Essential: Consistently applying risk management techniques, such as stop-losses and position sizing, helps maintain a disciplined trading approach.

5. Review and Adjust Your Risk Plan Regularly: Regularly assess and update your risk management strategies to adapt to changing market conditions and protect your trading capital effectively.

Conclusion

In the world of futures trading, where volatility can swing fortunes in an instant, mastering risk management is not just a strategy—it's a necessity. As we've explored, employing tools like stop-loss orders and precise position sizing allows traders to safeguard their capital against unexpected market shifts. Just as a captain steers a ship through turbulent waters with a steady hand and vigilant eye, so too must traders navigate the futures market with disciplined risk controls. By setting clear stop-loss levels and carefully sizing positions, you create a buffer that shields your investments from catastrophic losses, ensuring that even in the stormiest seas, your financial ship remains afloat. Remember, in futures trading, the real victory lies not in avoiding risk entirely, but in managing it with wisdom and foresight.

Chapter 9: Control Risk in Options

Introduction

In the dynamic world of stock market trading, options can be a powerful tool, but they also come with their own set of risks. In this chapter, we'll explore strategies designed to help you manage these risks effectively. We'll focus on defined-risk techniques like covered calls and protective puts, which are specifically crafted to help you safeguard your investments while still taking advantage of potential gains. By understanding and applying these strategies, you'll be better equipped to navigate the complexities of options trading with greater confidence and control over your financial outcomes.

Mastering Risk Control in Options Trading

Options trading can provide the opportunity for substantial gains, but it also involves inherent risks. To assist you in navigating this intricate field, we will explore defined-risk strategies. These strategies are designed to help manage risk while aiming to maximize potential profits. Here, we'll focus on two key strategies: Covered Calls and Protective Puts.

A) Covered Calls

Overview: A Covered Call strategy involves holding a long position in a stock and selling call options on that same stock. This strategy generates additional income from the premiums received from selling the call options.

In-Depth Analysis:

- Income Generation: By selling call options, you earn a premium upfront. This income can offset potential losses or enhance overall returns on your stock.

- Limited Upside: The maximum profit is capped because you're obligated to sell the stock at the strike price of the call option. If the stock price rises above this strike price, you won't benefit from the additional gains beyond the strike price.

- Downside Protection: The premium received from selling the call option provides a cushion against potential losses in the underlying stock.

Key Strategies:

- Selecting the Strike Price: Choose a strike price that reflects your willingness to sell the stock. Higher strike prices offer more potential upside but lower premiums, while lower strike prices offer higher premiums but limit your potential upside.

- Timing: Sell call options with expiration dates that align with your investment horizon. Short-term options offer higher premiums but require more frequent management.

Benefits:

- Increased Income: Premiums from selling call options boost your overall returns.

- Downside Cushion: The premium provides a buffer against minor declines in the stock price.

Example:

- Scenario: You own 100 shares of XYZ Corp at $50 per share. You sell a call option with a strike price of $55 for a premium of $2 per share.

- Outcome: If XYZ Corp rises to $55 or above, you sell your shares at $55, plus the $2 premium, totalling $57 per share. If the stock stays below $55, you keep the premium and can repeat the process.

B) Protective Puts

Overview: A Protective Put strategy involves buying a put option while holding a long position in the underlying stock. This acts as insurance against a significant decline in the stock price.

In-Depth Analysis:

- Downside Protection: The put option gives you the right to sell your stock at the strike price, limiting your potential losses.

- Cost: The premium paid for the put option is an added cost, which can reduce your overall profit if the stock price remains stable or rises.

- Flexibility: This strategy allows you to benefit from stock price appreciation while providing protection against sharp declines.

Key Strategies:

- Choosing the Right Strike Price: Select a strike price for the put option that balances cost with the level of protection you desire. A lower strike price is cheaper but offers less protection.

- Expiration Date: Choose an expiration date that aligns with your investment time frame. Longer expirations provide extended protection but come at a higher cost.

Benefits:

- Limited Losses: The put option ensures that your losses are capped if the stock price falls below the strike price.

- Profit Potential: You can still benefit from price increases in the underlying stock, while having a safety net in place.

Example:

- Scenario: You own 100 shares of ABC Inc. at $60 per share. You buy a put option with a strike price of $55 for a premium of $3 per share.

- Outcome: If ABC Inc. drops below $55, you can sell your shares at $55, limiting your losses to $5 per share (the difference between your purchase price and the strike price, plus the premium). If the stock price rises, you benefit from the appreciation minus the cost of the put.

Summary of Benefits

Covered Calls:

- Increased Income: Earn additional returns through option premiums.

- Downside Cushion: Premiums provide some protection against stock declines.

- Predictable Outcomes: Clear understanding of profit and loss limits.

Protective Puts:

- Downside Protection: Limits potential losses with a defined safety net.

- Profit Potential: Allows for gains if the stock price rises.

- Peace of Mind: Provides insurance against significant declines.

By mastering these defined-risk strategies, you can navigate the complexities of options trading with greater confidence, balancing risk and reward effectively.

Key Takeaways

1. Understand the Risks: Options trading can be volatile, but using defined-risk strategies helps you manage and limit potential losses.

2. Covered Calls: This strategy involves holding a stock and selling call options on it, providing extra income while capping your maximum gain.

3. Protective Puts: Buying put options on a stock you own acts as insurance, limiting potential losses if the stock price falls.

4. Balance Risk and Reward: Defined-risk strategies help balance the potential for profit

with the risk of loss, making your trading approach more predictable.

5. Stay Informed and Flexible: Continuously monitor your options positions and be ready to adjust strategies based on market conditions to keep risks under control.

Conclusion

In the world of options trading, where potential profits can be tantalizing, managing risk is crucial for sustained success. This chapter has explored defined-risk strategies like covered calls and protective puts, which act as financial safety nets, allowing traders to navigate the market with greater confidence. Just as a skilled sailor relies on a well-maintained ship to weather the storm, savvy options traders use these strategies to mitigate risk and safeguard their investments. By understanding and applying these tools, you can better harness the power of options while keeping potential losses in check, turning uncertainty into opportunity.

Chapter 10: Leverage Futures for Profit

Introduction

Welcome to the thrilling world of futures trading, where opportunity meets risk on a grand scale. In this chapter, we'll unravel the complexities of leveraging futures contracts to boost your investment potential. Imagine a high-stakes game where your bets can lead to impressive gains or significant losses, all depending on how well you manage your margins and funds. We'll break down the essentials of margin requirements, the importance of keeping a safety cushion, and the inherent risks of using high leverage. By mastering these elements, you'll be better equipped to navigate the fast-paced futures market and turn its challenges into lucrative opportunities.

Maximizing Profits with Futures: Mastering Leverage and Risk

A) Understanding Futures and Leverage

Futures Trading Overview: Futures contracts are agreements to buy or sell an asset at a predetermined price on a future date. Leverage in futures trading allows you to control a large position with a relatively small amount of capital, amplifying both potential profits and losses.

i) Key Concepts

    1. Margin Requirements:

- Definition: Margin is the initial amount of money required to open a futures position. It acts as a security deposit.

- Types of Margin:

  - Initial Margin: The upfront amount needed to enter a trade.

  - Maintenance Margin: The minimum balance required to keep a position open. If your account falls below this level, you'll get a margin call to deposit more funds.

2. Leverage Impact:

- Magnified Gains: Leverage allows you to control a larger position with a smaller amount of money. For example, with 10x leverage, a 1% increase in the asset's price can lead to a 10% gain on your invested capital.

- Magnified Losses: Similarly, losses are also magnified. A 1% drop in the asset's price could result in a 10% loss on your capital.

3. Risk Management:

- Importance: High leverage increases both potential profits and risks. Proper risk management strategies are crucial to protect your capital.

- Tools: Use stop-loss orders and limit orders to control potential losses and secure profits.

ii) Strategies for Effective Futures Trading

- Understand Your Leverage:
    - Calculate Risk: Always calculate the total amount at risk based on your leverage and ensure it aligns with your risk tolerance.
    - Adjust Leverage: Use lower leverage if you're less experienced or if market conditions are volatile.

- Maintain Adequate Margin:
    - Monitor Your Account: Regularly check your margin levels to avoid margin calls and potential forced liquidation of your position.
    - Set Aside Funds: Keep additional funds in reserve to cover margin requirements and unexpected market movements.

- Implement Risk Management Techniques:
    - Stop-Loss Orders: Set stop-loss orders to automatically exit a position if the price moves against you beyond a certain point.
    - Take-Profit Orders: Use take-profit orders to lock in gains when the price hits a desired level.

iii) Examples

- Example 1:
  - Scenario: You use 10x leverage to buy a futures contract worth $100,000 with only $10,000 margin.
  - Outcome: If the asset's price rises by 5%, your contract's value increases by $5,000, translating to a 50% gain on your margin. Conversely, a 5% drop would result in a 50% loss.
- Example 2:
  - Scenario: You trade with a 5x leverage and place a stop-loss order at a 2% loss threshold.
  - Outcome: If the market moves against you by 2%, the stop-loss order helps you exit the position, limiting your loss to 10% of your capital (2% of the 5x leveraged position).

iv) Benefits of Leveraged Futures Trading

- Increased Profit Potential:
  - Higher Returns: With leverage, small price movements can lead to significant gains.
  - Efficient Use of Capital: Control large positions without needing the full amount of capital.
- Enhanced Flexibility:

- Diverse Strategies: Use leverage to implement various trading strategies like hedging, speculating, or arbitraging.

- Opportunity for Diversification:

    - Access to Different Markets: Leverage allows you to explore and invest in multiple futures markets with a smaller capital base.

v) Final Thoughts

Leveraging futures can be a powerful tool for increasing your potential profits, but it comes with significant risks. Understanding margin requirements, maintaining adequate funds, and implementing effective risk management strategies are essential for navigating the complexities of futures trading successfully. By managing leverage wisely and using protective measures, you can harness the benefits of futures trading while minimizing potential downsides.

Key Takeaways

1. Leverage Amplifies Results: Futures trading uses leverage to amplify potential gains, but it also magnifies potential losses, so caution is crucial.

2. Understand Margin Requirements: Knowing the margin requirements is essential; it determines how much capital you need to control a larger position.

3. Maintain Sufficient Funds: Always keep extra funds in your account to cover margin calls and avoid forced liquidation during market volatility.

4. Risk Management is Key: Employ strategies like stop-loss orders and position sizing to manage the inherent risks of high leverage.

5. Educate Yourself Thoroughly: A solid understanding of how leverage works and its impact on your trades can significantly improve your trading outcomes.

Conclusion

In the world of stock market trading, leveraging futures offers the tantalizing potential for substantial profits, but it comes with a high degree of risk. This chapter has illuminated the dual-edged nature of leverage, where the same tool that can amplify gains can equally magnify losses. As we've explored, managing margin requirements and ensuring you have ample funds are not just best practices—they're crucial to safeguarding your investments. In essence, while futures trading can be a powerful strategy for those who navigate its complexities wisely, it is paramount to approach it with caution and a clear understanding of the risks involved. As the saying goes, "In investing, what is comfortable is rarely profitable," so equip yourself with knowledge and strategy to transform leverage from a risky speculation into a strategic advantage.

Chapter 11: Utilize Options for Income

Introduction

Welcome to a world where your investments can work even harder for you. In this chapter, we'll dive into the fascinating realm of options trading, focusing on how selling options can become a steady source of income. Imagine having a powerful tool that not only allows you to generate extra cash but also helps manage risk with finesse. We'll break down strategies like writing covered calls—where you sell options against stocks you already own—to unlock consistent income streams. Whether you're new to this concept or looking to refine your approach, you'll learn how to leverage these techniques to enhance your financial stability.

Unlocking Steady Income with Options

Options trading can be a powerful tool for generating income in the stock market. By selling options, particularly covered calls, investors can earn premium income while managing risk. This strategy leverages the potential of options to provide a consistent revenue stream. Let's break down how it works, its benefits, and key strategies to maximize its effectiveness.

What Are Covered Calls?

A covered call strategy involves selling call options on stocks you already own. Here's a step-by-step breakdown:

1. Own the Stock: You must first own shares of a stock in your portfolio.

2. Sell a Call Option: Sell (or "write") a call option on the stock you own. This gives the buyer the right, but not the obligation, to purchase the stock from you at a predetermined price (the strike price) before a specific date (the expiration date).

3. Collect Premium: You receive a premium from selling the call option. This premium is your income.

In-Depth Analysis of Covered Calls

1. Income Generation:

   - Premium Collection: When you sell a call option, you collect a premium upfront. This is immediate income, which can enhance your portfolio's overall returns.

   - Regular Cash Flow: By employing covered calls consistently, you can create a regular income stream, especially in a stable or slightly bullish market.

2. Risk Management:

   - Stock Ownership: Since you already own the underlying stock, your risk is limited to the stock's performance rather than the full risk associated with buying options outright.

   - Premium Buffer: The premium you receive provides a cushion against potential losses if the stock price falls, effectively lowering your break-even point.

3. Potential Upside Limitation:

- Cap on Gains: The maximum profit is capped at the strike price plus the premium received. If the stock price rises significantly above the strike price, you may miss out on some of those gains because you are obligated to sell the stock at the strike price if the option is exercised.

Key Strategies for Success

1. Selecting the Right Strike Price:

- In-the-Money vs. Out-of-the-Money: Choosing an out-of-the-money strike price can allow for potential stock price appreciation while still generating premium income. In-the-money strikes may offer higher premiums but limit upside potential.

- Balance Risk and Reward: Aim for a strike price that aligns with your market outlook and income goals.

2. Expiration Date Considerations:

- Short-Term vs. Long-Term: Short-term options provide more frequent premium income opportunities but require more active management. Long-term options reduce the frequency of trades but may offer less frequent premium collections.

3. Market Conditions:

- Volatility: Higher market volatility generally leads to higher option premiums. Selling covered calls in a volatile market can increase income potential.

- Stock Performance: Regularly review the stock's performance and adjust your strategy based on market conditions and your investment goals.

Examples and Benefits

- Example 1: You own 100 shares of XYZ Corporation, currently trading at $50. You sell a call option with a strike price of $55, expiring in one month, and receive a $2 premium. If XYZ stays below $55, you keep the premium as income. If XYZ rises above $55, you sell your shares at $55, plus the $2 premium, capturing both gains and income.

- Example 2: You own 200 shares of ABC Inc., trading at $75. You sell two call options with a $80 strike price, earning $3 per share in premiums. If ABC remains below $80, you keep the premium. If it rises above $80, you sell your shares at $80 each, plus the $3 premium per share.

Benefits of Covered Calls

- Increased Income: Regular premiums add to your overall portfolio return.

- Reduced Risk: Premium income provides a buffer against stock price declines.

- Controlled Returns: Aligns with a strategy of stable, predictable returns.

By effectively utilizing covered calls, you can enhance your income while managing risk and achieving your investment objectives.

Key Takeaways

1. Generate Income through Premiums: Selling options lets you earn money upfront by collecting premiums from buyers, adding a steady income stream to your investment strategy.

2. Covered Calls Simplified: Writing covered calls involves selling call options on stocks you own, allowing you to earn additional income while potentially capping your upside.

3. Balancing Risk and Reward: Strategies like covered calls can help manage risk by providing income, but they may limit your potential gains if the stock price rises significantly.

4. Consistency with Strategy: Regularly employing option-selling strategies can provide a consistent income stream, especially if you choose reliable stocks and manage your positions carefully.

5. Understanding Market Conditions: Success in selling options depends on market conditions and stock performance, so it's crucial to stay informed and adjust your strategies accordingly.

Conclusion

In the dynamic realm of the stock market, utilizing options to generate income is akin to having a strategic tool in your financial toolkit. By selling options, particularly through strategies like writing covered calls, you can earn premiums that add a steady stream of income to your portfolio. This approach not only offers a way to enhance your earnings but also helps manage risk by allowing you to leverage assets you already own. As Warren Buffett wisely said, "The stock market is designed to transfer money from the Active to the Patient." Embracing these options strategies can turn your patience into profit, demonstrating that with the right techniques, even the stock market's volatility can become a source of opportunity.

Chapter 12: Track Market Trends and Data

Introduction

In the ever-changing world of stock markets, staying ahead of the game requires more than just intuition—it demands a keen eye for tracking market trends, economic indicators, and breaking news. This chapter delves into the crucial art of monitoring these elements, offering clear guidance on where to find reliable data and how to interpret it to make well-informed trading decisions. By understanding the flow of market trends and the impact of economic signals, you'll be better equipped to navigate the complexities of investing and capitalize on opportunities with confidence.

Mastering Market Trends: A Global Perspective on Informed Trading Decisions

A) Understanding Market Trends and Data

Success in trading requires a deep understanding of market trends and data. This guide will focus on both the Indian stock market and five major global stock markets, helping you make well-informed trading decisions.

a) Indian Stock Market Overview

1. Nifty 50

- Description: The Nifty 50 is a stock market index representing 50 of the largest and most liquid stocks listed on the National Stock Exchange (NSE) of India.

- Benefit: Tracking the Nifty 50 gives you insights into the overall health of the Indian stock market, reflecting the performance of leading companies across various sectors.

2. Sensex

- Description: The Sensex (Sensitive Index) comprises 30 of the largest and most actively traded stocks on the Bombay Stock Exchange (BSE).

- Benefit: Like the Nifty 50, the Sensex provides a snapshot of the Indian economy's performance, helping investors gauge market trends and sentiment.

3. Economic Indicators for India

- Examples: GDP growth rate, inflation rate, and industrial production index.

- Benefit: Understanding these indicators helps you anticipate changes in market conditions and adjust your investment strategies accordingly.

4. Company Reports and News

- Examples: Corporate earnings reports, policy changes, and major economic reforms.

- Benefit: Staying updated on these factors helps you make informed decisions based on a company's performance and broader economic policies.

B) Key Strategies for the Indian Stock Market

1. Monitor RBI Policies

- Strategy: Follow updates on the Reserve Bank of India's (RBI) monetary policies and interest rate changes.

- Example: An increase in interest rates might negatively impact consumer spending and company profits, affecting stock prices.

- Benefit: RBI policies influence market liquidity and economic conditions, crucial for making timely trading decisions.

2. Track Government Announcements

- Strategy: Stay informed about government budgets, reforms, and economic policies.

- Example: A new infrastructure development plan could boost stocks in the construction and materials sectors.

- Benefit: Government decisions can create investment opportunities or risks, impacting various sectors differently.

C) Global Stock Markets Overview

1. United States: S&P 500

- Description: The S&P 500 is a stock market index that includes 500 of the largest companies listed on stock exchanges in the U.S.

- Benefit: This index provides a broad view of the U.S. economy and is a benchmark for global investors.

2. China: Shanghai Composite

- Description: The Shanghai Composite Index tracks all the stocks listed on the Shanghai Stock Exchange.

- Benefit: This index reflects the performance of China's largest companies and can signal trends in the Chinese economy.

3. Japan: Nikkei 225

- Description: The Nikkei 225 consists of 225 large Japanese companies listed on the Tokyo Stock Exchange.

- Benefit: It provides insights into Japan's economic health and market trends, which can influence global markets.

4. Germany: DAX 30

- Description: The DAX 30 includes 30 major German companies traded on the Frankfurt Stock Exchange.

- Benefit: Tracking the DAX 30 helps understand economic conditions in Europe's largest economy and its impact on global markets.

5. United Kingdom: FTSE 100

- Description: The FTSE 100 represents the 100 largest companies listed on the London Stock Exchange.

- Benefit: This index provides insights into the performance of the UK's largest companies and reflects broader economic trends in the region.

D) Strategies for Global Market Trends

1. Follow Global Economic News

- Strategy: Keep an eye on global economic news, such as trade policies, geopolitical events, and international economic reports.

- Example: Trade tensions between major economies can affect global markets and individual stock performance.

- Benefit: Staying updated on global news helps you understand how international events might impact your investments.

2. Analyze Currency Fluctuations

- Strategy: Monitor currency exchange rates and their impact on multinational companies.

- Example: A strong U.S. dollar can impact the profitability of U.S. companies with significant international sales.

- Benefit: Currency movements can affect global trade and investment returns, making it crucial to consider in your trading strategy.

3. Diversify Across Global Markets

- Strategy: Invest in a mix of stocks from different countries and regions.

- Example: Combining investments in the U.S., Europe, and Asia can reduce risk and capitalize on growth opportunities in various markets.

- Benefit: Diversification helps spread risk and can improve overall portfolio performance by tapping into different economic conditions.

4. Utilize International Index Funds

- Strategy: Invest in index funds or ETFs that track global markets or specific regions.

- Example: Investing in a global ETF allows you to gain exposure to multiple international markets without having to select individual stocks.

- Benefit: Index funds offer diversified exposure and can simplify the process of investing in global markets.

E) Overall Summary

Mastering market trends and data interpretation is essential for successful trading. By focusing on key indices, economic indicators, and global news, you can make informed decisions in both the Indian and global stock markets. Use these strategies to stay ahead of market trends, diversify your investments, and optimize your trading approach for better outcomes.

Key Takeaways

- Global and Local Insights: Keep an eye on both Indian and global market trends to understand the interconnected nature of economies and stock movements.

- Reliable Data Sources: Use trusted financial news websites, official reports, and market data platforms for accurate and timely information.

- Trend Analysis: Recognize and analyze recurring market patterns to anticipate future stock price movements and investment opportunities.

- Economic Indicators: Track key economic indicators like interest rates, inflation, and GDP growth, as they significantly influence market behaviour.

- Data Integration: Combine insights from various data sources and indicators to create a well-rounded view, enhancing your trading strategies and decisions.

Conclusion

Tracking market trends and data is crucial for making smart trading decisions in both the Indian and global stock markets. Just as a navigator uses stars to guide their journey, traders rely on market trends, economic indicators, and news to chart their path. This chapter has explored various sources of market data, emphasizing the importance of not just collecting information, but also interpreting it with insight and clarity. By understanding how these trends and indicators influence market movements, you can better anticipate shifts and make informed decisions. Remember, as Peter Lynch wisely said, "The stock market is filled with individuals who know the price of everything, but the value of nothing." Equip yourself with the knowledge to discern the value behind the numbers, and you'll steer your investments with confidence and precision.

Chapter 13: Analyze Stock Market Volatility

Introduction

In the world of stock markets, volatility is like the heartbeat of trading—constant, fluctuating, and essential. It represents the degree of variation in the price of a stock over time, influencing how traders perceive risk and opportunity. In this chapter, we'll dive into the concept of implied volatility, which reveals market expectations about future price swings and plays a pivotal role in determining option prices. Understanding this dynamic will empower you to navigate options trading with greater insight, allowing you to harness volatility to enhance your strategies and make more informed decisions. Whether you're a seasoned trader or just starting out, mastering the art of analyzing stock market volatility will give you a significant edge in the ever-changing landscape of options trading.

Navigating Stock Market Volatility: A Guide to Mastering Options Trading

Understanding stock market volatility is crucial for anyone involved in options trading. Here's an in-depth look at how volatility affects options, with strategies to harness it effectively:

1. What is Stock Market Volatility?

Definition: Volatility refers to the degree of variation in a stock's price over time. It measures how much and how quickly a stock's price fluctuates. High volatility means large price swings, while low volatility indicates steadier price movements.

Impact on Options Trading:

- Options Premiums: Volatility influences the price of options. Higher volatility generally leads to higher option premiums because the potential for significant price movements increases the likelihood of the option becoming profitable.

- Risk and Reward: Greater volatility can increase potential rewards but also raises risk. Traders must weigh these factors when deciding on trades.

Example: Imagine Stock A typically fluctuates between $50 and $55. If news causes the stock to jump to $60 or drop to $40, it shows high volatility. An option trader could benefit from this volatility if they anticipate further price movements.

2. Implied Volatility (IV) Explained

Definition: Implied volatility is the market's forecast of a stock's future volatility, derived from the prices of options. It reflects the market's expectations and is not based on historical data.

Impact on Option Pricing:

- Higher IV: Increases option premiums. Traders might pay more for options because the market expects larger price movements.

- Lower IV: Decreases option premiums. Options are cheaper but might not be as lucrative if price movements are less significant.

Example: If an option on Stock B has a high IV, its price might be higher due to expectations of large price swings. Conversely, if the IV is low, the option price might be lower, reflecting expectations of minimal movement.

3. Strategies to Leverage Volatility

A. Straddle Strategy

- What It Is: Buying both a call and a put option on the same stock with the same strike price and expiration date.

- When to Use: Ideal when anticipating significant price movement but unsure of the direction.

- Benefit: Profits if the stock price moves significantly in either direction.

B. Strangle Strategy

- What It Is: Buying a call option and a put option with different strike prices but the same expiration date.

- When to Use: When expecting significant price movement but wanting to lower the cost compared to a straddle.

- Benefit: Profits from large price movements with lower upfront costs compared to a straddle.

C. Iron Condor Strategy

- What It Is: Selling an out-of-the-money call and put option while buying a further out-of-the-money call and put option.

- When to Use: When expecting low volatility and minimal price movement.

- Benefit: Limited risk and potential profit in a stable market.

D. Calendar Spread Strategy

- What It Is: Buying and selling call or put options with the same strike price but different expiration dates.

- When to Use: When expecting volatility in the near term but less so in the long term.

- Benefit: Takes advantage of differences in time decay and volatility over different periods.

4. Key Insights

- Monitor IV Trends: Regularly track changes in implied volatility to make informed decisions. Significant increases or decreases can signal trading opportunities.

- Use Volatility Tools: Utilize tools like the VIX (Volatility Index) to gauge overall market volatility and its potential impact on options.

- Risk Management: Always implement proper risk management strategies to protect against unexpected market movements.

Benefits:

- Informed Decision-Making: Understanding volatility helps in making strategic trading choices.

- Optimized Returns: Leveraging volatility can enhance potential returns while managing risks effectively.

- Strategic Flexibility: Various strategies allow traders to adapt to different market conditions, whether they anticipate high or low volatility.

By mastering these concepts and strategies, traders can navigate the complexities of stock market volatility, enhancing their options trading success.

Key Takeaways

1. Volatility Basics: Volatility measures the extent of price fluctuations in a stock, indicating how much and how quickly the price moves up and down.

2. Implied Volatility Explained: Implied volatility (IV) reflects the market's forecast of a stock's potential movement and is derived from options pricing.

3. Impact on Option Pricing: High implied volatility generally increases option premiums, as it suggests a greater likelihood of significant price changes.

4. Leveraging Volatility: Traders can use volatility to their advantage by employing strategies like

straddles or strangles, which profit from large price swings.

5. Risk Management: Understanding and anticipating volatility helps in managing risk, as it allows traders to adjust their positions and strategies based on expected market movements.

Conclusion

In the world of options trading, volatility is like the heartbeat of the market, controlling how prices go up and down. This chapter explains volatility and shows how it greatly affects option prices and trading decisions. As Warren Buffett wisely observed, "Volatility is far from synonymous with risk," emphasizing that understanding and leveraging this volatility can be the key to unlocking significant opportunities. Just as a skilled sailor reads the winds to navigate through stormy seas, traders who comprehend volatility can expertly chart their course, transforming market uncertainty into a strategic advantage. By mastering the nuances of volatility, traders can not only anticipate market shifts but also strategically position themselves to capitalize on these fluctuations, ultimately turning potential challenges into pathways for success.

Chapter 14: Use Technical Analysis

Introduction

Welcome to the world of Technical Analysis, where the art of predicting stock market movements meets the science of charts and indicators. Imagine you have a crystal ball that doesn't show the future directly but instead provides clues about where prices might head based on past patterns. In this chapter, we'll unlock the secrets of technical analysis by diving into essential tools and techniques that traders use to forecast market trends. From understanding chart patterns to interpreting key indicators, you'll learn how to harness these powerful tools to make informed decisions in futures and options trading, transforming complex data into actionable insights. Whether you're a novice or looking to refine your trading strategy, this guide will equip you with the knowledge to navigate the market with confidence.

Mastering Technical Analysis: Essential Tools for Predicting Market Movements

Technical analysis is a powerful method used to forecast stock price movements by analyzing historical data and chart patterns. For traders dealing in futures and options, understanding technical analysis is crucial for making informed decisions. Here's a breakdown of key tools and strategies in technical analysis:

1. Chart Patterns

Definition: Chart patterns are formations on stock price charts that tend to repeat over time. These patterns can signal potential future movements.

Popular Patterns:

- Head and Shoulders: Indicates a reversal in trend.
- Double Top/Bottom: Shows potential reversal points.
- Triangles (Ascending, Descending, Symmetrical): Signal continuation or reversal depending on the breakout direction.

Benefits:

- Predict Market Reversals: Helps identify potential turning points in the market.
- Spot Trends Early: Provides signals on whether the trend is likely to continue or change.

Example:

- Head and Shoulders Formation: A classic pattern where a peak (head) is flanked by two smaller peaks (shoulders). A head and shoulders top indicates a potential bearish reversal, while an inverse pattern suggests a bullish reversal.

2. Technical Indicators

Definition: Indicators are mathematical calculations based on historical price, volume, or open interest data. They help in analyzing trends, momentum, and market volatility.

Key Indicators:

- Moving Averages (MA): Smooth out price data to identify the direction of the trend. E.g., Simple Moving Average (SMA), Exponential Moving Average (EMA).

- Relative Strength Index (RSI): Measures the speed and change of price movements to identify overbought or oversold conditions.

- Moving Average Convergence Divergence (MACD): Shows the relationship between two moving averages of a security's price.

Benefits:

- Trend Identification: Helps traders understand the direction of the market.

- Entry and Exit Points: Indicators can signal optimal times to buy or sell.

Example:

- RSI: If the RSI is above 70, the stock may be overbought and could be due for a pull back. If below 30, it might be oversold and due for a bounce.

3. Volume Analysis

Definition: Volume refers to the number of shares or contracts traded in a security or market. Analyzing volume can provide insights into the strength of a price move.

Key Concepts:

- Volume Spikes: Large increases in volume often accompany significant price moves and can indicate a trend's strength or a reversal.

- Volume and Price Relationship: Increasing volume with rising prices confirms an uptrend, while increasing volume with falling prices confirms a downtrend.

Benefits:

- Confirm Trends: Helps verify whether a trend is strong or weakening.

- Predict Reversals: Can signal potential reversals when volume changes significantly.

Example:

- Volume Surge During a Breakout: If a stock breaks out of a resistance level with high volume, it suggests strong investor interest and a higher probability of sustained movement.

4. Support and Resistance Levels

Definition: Support and resistance levels are horizontal lines drawn on a chart where the price tends to stop and reverse. Support is where the price typically finds a floor, while resistance is where it faces a ceiling.

Benefits:

- Trade Planning: Helps in setting entry and exit points.

- Risk Management: Useful for placing stop-loss orders to minimize losses.

Example:

- Support Level: If a stock repeatedly bounces back from a price level, this level is considered support. Traders may look to buy near this support level with the expectation that the price will bounce back.

Key Strategies for Using Technical Analysis

- Combine Indicators: Use multiple indicators to confirm signals. For example, combine RSI with moving averages to strengthen buy or sell decisions.

- Trend Following: Stick with the trend. Use moving averages to confirm trends and avoid trading against the prevailing direction.

- Risk Management: Always use stop-loss orders to protect against unexpected market movements.

- Back testing: Test strategies on historical data to ensure they have a positive performance track record before applying them in live trading.

By mastering these technical analysis tools and strategies, traders can enhance their ability to predict market movements and make more informed decisions in futures and options trading.

Key Takeaways

1. Technical Indicators: Key tools like Moving Averages and Relative Strength Index (RSI) help forecast market trends by analyzing historical price data.

2. Chart Patterns: Recognizing patterns such as Head and Shoulders or Double Tops can signal potential market reversals and trends.

3. Support and Resistance: Identifying price levels where markets tend to reverse helps in setting entry and exit points for trades.

4. Volume Analysis: Examining trading volume alongside price movements reveals the strength of trends and can confirm market signals.

5. Risk Management: Combining technical analysis with proper risk management strategies ensures informed decision-making and limits potential losses.

Conclusion

Technical analysis serves as a vital compass for navigating the stock market's turbulent waters. By leveraging indicators and chart patterns, traders gain invaluable insights into potential price movements, turning abstract data into actionable strategies. Just as a skilled navigator reads the stars to chart a course, technical analysis deciphers market signals to guide futures and options trading decisions. Embracing the idea that "knowledge is power," mastering these techniques helps traders navigate market uncertainties with confidence, turning challenges into opportunities and achieving their financial goals more effectively.

Chapter 15: Implement Risk Management

Introduction

In the bustling world of stock market investing, managing risk is like steering a ship through unpredictable waters. This chapter delves into essential techniques for safeguarding your investments, with a focus on navigating the complexities of futures and options trading. We'll explore key strategies such as short selling, where you bet on declining stock prices, and compare this with other vital tools like stop-loss orders, which help limit potential losses, and portfolio diversification, which spreads out risk by holding a variety of investments. By understanding and applying these risk management techniques, you'll be better equipped to protect your investments and sail towards your financial goals with greater confidence.

Mastering Risk Management in Stock Market Trading

Effective risk management is essential for anyone involved in stock market trading. It helps in protecting your investments from significant losses while maximizing potential gains. In this chapter, we'll delve into key risk management techniques, focusing on the differences between short selling, stop-loss orders, and portfolio diversification. We will also explore strategies to mitigate risks in futures and options trading.

1. Short Selling vs. Stop-Loss Orders

Short Selling

- Definition: Short selling involves borrowing shares of a stock that you don't own, selling them at the current market price, and then buying them back later at a lower price to return to the lender. The aim is to profit from a decline in the stock's price.

- Risks:

  - Unlimited Losses: Theoretically, a stock's price can rise indefinitely, meaning potential losses can be limitless.

  - Margin Calls: If the stock price increases, you may be required to deposit additional funds to maintain your position.

  - Regulatory Risks: Short selling can be restricted or banned during periods of high volatility.

Stop-Loss Orders

- Definition: A stop-loss order is a pre-set order to sell a security when it reaches a certain price, designed to limit an investor's loss.

- Risks:

  - Market Gaps: In fast-moving markets, the stop price may be exceeded before the order is executed, leading to higher losses than anticipated.

  - False Alarms: The stock price might briefly dip below the stop price before rising again, causing unnecessary sales.

Benefits of Stop-Loss Orders:

- Controlled Losses: Limits the amount of loss you can incur on a trade.

- Automatic Execution: Executes trades automatically once the stop price is reached, removing emotional decision-making.

- Peace of Mind: Helps manage risk without constant monitoring of the market.

Benefits of Short Selling:

- Profit from Declines: Allows you to profit from falling stock prices, potentially hedging against market downturns.

- Flexibility: Can be used in various market conditions and strategies.

Key Strategy for Managing Risks:

- Combining Both: Use stop-loss orders to protect against significant losses while employing short selling strategies to capitalize on falling stock prices.

2. Portfolio Diversification

Definition:

- Portfolio diversification involves spreading investments across various asset classes (stocks, bonds, real estate, etc.) to reduce the overall risk.

Benefits:

- Risk Reduction: By holding a mix of assets, you lower the impact of any single investment's poor performance on your overall portfolio.

- Smoother Returns: Diversified portfolios tend to have more stable returns over time because different assets respond differently to market events.

- Increased Opportunity: Exposure to various sectors and asset classes can capture gains from different market segments.

Key Strategy for Diversification:

- Asset Allocation: Allocate investments across various asset classes based on risk tolerance, investment goals, and market conditions.

- Regular Rebalancing: Periodically adjust your portfolio to maintain your desired asset allocation and risk level.

3. Risk Management in Futures and Options Trading

Futures Trading

- Definition: Futures are contracts to buy or sell an asset at a future date at a predetermined price.

- Risks:

  - Leverage: Futures contracts often involve high leverage, meaning small price changes can result in significant gains or losses.

- Margin Requirements: You may be required to maintain a margin, and failing to do so can lead to forced liquidation.

Options Trading

- Definition: Options are contracts that give the right, but not the obligation, to buy (call) or sell (put) an asset at a specified price before the contract expires.

- Risks:

    - Time Decay: The value of options decreases as they approach expiration, potentially resulting in losses if the underlying asset does not move as expected.

    - Complex Strategies: Options trading involves complex strategies and pricing models, increasing the risk of misjudgment.

Strategies for Managing Risks in Futures and Options:

- Hedging: Use futures and options to hedge against adverse movements in other investments or positions.

- Limit Orders: Use limit orders to manage entry and exit points effectively.

- Position Sizing: Avoid excessive leverage by sizing positions according to your risk tolerance and account balance.

- Education and Practice: Gain a thorough understanding of futures and options through education and simulated trading before committing real capital.

By understanding and applying these risk management techniques, you can protect your investments and navigate the stock market with greater confidence and effectiveness.

Key Takeaways

1. Understand Short Selling: Short selling involves betting that a stock's price will fall, but it carries high risk if the price rises unexpectedly.

2. Use Stop-Loss Orders: Stop-loss orders automatically sell a stock at a predetermined price to limit potential losses.

3. Diversify Your Portfolio: Spread investments across different assets to reduce the impact of a single asset's poor performance.

4. Leverage Risk Management in Futures: In futures trading, use strategies like setting strict loss limits to protect against significant losses due to market fluctuations.

5. Apply Options Strategies Wisely: Utilize options for hedging or leveraging positions, but ensure you understand the potential risks and rewards involved.

Conclusion

In the world of stock market investing, mastering risk management is not just a precaution—it's a cornerstone of success. Just as a skilled sailor uses both the compass and the anchor to navigate treacherous waters, savvy investors employ tools like stop-loss orders and portfolio diversification to safeguard their investments. As Warren Buffett wisely advised, "Risk comes from not knowing what you're doing." By adopting risk management strategies, investors can protect themselves against unforeseen market fluctuations and enhance their chances of long-term success. Remember, "It is not the strongest of the species that survive, nor the most intelligent, but the one most responsive to change." Embracing effective risk management ensures you stay resilient and adaptable, ready to thrive in the ever-

Chapter 16: Adapt to Market Conditions

Introduction

In the ever-changing world of stock markets, success hinges not just on having a solid strategy, but on the ability to adapt it as conditions shift. Just as weather forecasts guide us to dress appropriately for the day, understanding and reacting to market dynamics can significantly influence your trading results. This chapter delves into the art of adapting your trading strategies in response to economic events, emerging market trends, and fresh information, ensuring that your approach remains effective and resilient regardless of market fluctuations. By staying agile and informed, you'll turn challenges into opportunities and enhance your potential for success in the stock market.

Adapting Your Stock Market Strategy: Staying Ahead of the Curve

In the ever-changing world of stock markets, adaptability is your best ally. As economic events, market trends, and new information emerge, your trading strategies need to adjust. Here's a detailed look at how to keep your approach effective and responsive:

1. Understanding Economic Events

In-Depth Analysis: Economic events like interest rate changes, inflation reports, and unemployment data significantly impact market behaviour. For instance, when the Federal Reserve raises interest rates, borrowing costs increase, which can slow down economic growth and affect stock prices.

Key Strategies:

- Monitor Economic Indicators: Stay updated on key reports and announcements.

- Adjust Investment Focus: Shift towards sectors that typically perform well under certain economic conditions (e.g., consumer staples during inflation).

Example: If a strong jobs report is released, signalling economic growth, consider investing in growth stocks that benefit from a booming economy. Conversely, during a recession, defensive stocks like utilities might be safer.

Benefits:

- Timely Adjustments: Align investments with economic conditions.

- Risk Management: Protect against adverse effects of economic downturns.

2. Tracking Market Trends

In-Depth Analysis: Market trends can be bullish (upward), bearish (downward), or sideways (flat). Identifying and following these trends helps in making informed decisions. Technical analysis tools, such as moving averages and trend lines, can aid in recognizing these patterns.

Key Strategies:

- Use Trend Indicators: Employ tools like moving averages or the Relative Strength Index (RSI) to identify trends.

- Follow Market Sentiment: Pay attention to news and investor sentiment that may influence market direction.

Example: During a bullish trend, investing in growth stocks or index funds may yield higher returns. In a bearish market, consider short-selling or investing in counter-cyclical sectors.

Benefits:

- Optimized Entry and Exit Points: Enhance timing for buying or selling stocks.

- Informed Decisions: Make strategic choices based on prevailing market conditions.

3. Incorporating New Information

In-Depth Analysis: New information, such as earnings reports, mergers and acquisitions, or geopolitical events, can cause significant price movements. Staying informed allows you to react promptly to such developments.

Key Strategies:

- Stay Updated with News: Follow financial news sources and updates from reliable platforms.

- Analyze Impact: Assess how new information might affect individual stocks or sectors.

Example: If a company announces a breakthrough product, its stock price may surge. Reacting swiftly by buying the stock before the news is fully absorbed can be advantageous.

Benefits:

- Proactive Investing: Capitalize on opportunities created by new developments.

- Enhanced Flexibility: Adapt your portfolio based on the latest information.

Overall Summary

A) Adapting Your Strategy:

- Combine Approaches: Integrate economic analysis, trend tracking, and new information to make holistic investment decisions.

- Be Agile: Adjust your strategy regularly to reflect current market conditions and personal financial goals.

B) Benefits:

- Increased Returns: By aligning your strategy with market realities, you can potentially increase returns.

- Reduced Risk: Adaptive strategies help in mitigating losses during unfavourable conditions.

By understanding and incorporating these strategies, you'll be better equipped to navigate the dynamic stock market and achieve your investment goals.

Key Takeaways

- Monitor Economic Indicators: Stay informed about key economic reports like GDP, inflation, and employment figures as they can signal market shifts and influence your trading strategy.

- Adjust to Market Trends: Regularly review market trends and pivot your strategies to align with prevailing movements, ensuring you're not stuck in outdated approaches.

- React to News and Events: Major news events and geopolitical developments can cause sudden market changes, so be prepared to adjust your trades and investments in response.

- Use Technical Analysis: Employ technical indicators and chart patterns to identify changes in market momentum and adapt your strategies accordingly.

- Stay Flexible: Embrace a mindset of flexibility and continual learning, as rigid strategies are less effective in a constantly evolving market environment.

Conclusion

In the ever-shifting world of the stock market, adaptability is your greatest asset. Just as a skilled sailor adjusts their sails to the changing winds, successful traders must continuously refine their strategies in response to economic events, market trends, and emerging data. This chapter underscores the importance of staying agile and informed, emphasizing that rigid approaches often lead to missed opportunities or increased risk. Embrace the dynamic nature of the market by staying educated and flexible, allowing your strategies to evolve with the tides of change. As the renowned investor As Warren Buffett wisely noted,

"Price is what you pay; value is what you get." By adapting to market conditions, you ensure that your trading approach not only aligns with current realities but also maximizes your potential for long-term success.

Chapter 17: Short Selling in Spot and Futures Market

Introduction

Welcome to our exploration of short selling in the stock market—a strategy that can offer both thrilling opportunities and significant risks. In this chapter, we will demystify short selling by comparing it with put options, unravel the regulations governing short trades, especially in the Indian and global futures and options markets, and outline essential elements to navigate this tactic legally and profitably. Whether you're looking to hedge against potential losses or capitalize on market downturns, understanding the nuances of short selling is crucial. We will guide you through the pros and cons, ensuring you gain a clear, actionable insight into making smart, informed trading decisions.

Short Selling in Spot and Futures Markets: Understanding the Basics

A) Short Selling: An Overview Short selling is a trading strategy where an investor sells a security they don't own, with the hope of buying it back at a lower price. This technique can be used in both spot (immediate delivery) and futures (contract-based delivery) markets.

B) Spot Market vs. Futures Market for Short Selling

- Spot Market: Involves buying and selling securities for immediate delivery. Short selling in the spot market means borrowing the stock, selling it at the current price, and then buying it back later at a lower price.

- Futures Market: Involves agreements to buy or sell an asset at a future date at an agreed-upon price. Short selling in futures involves selling a futures contract with the expectation that the asset's price will decline.

C) Pros and Cons of Short Selling

Pros:

- Profit from Declines: Allows traders to profit from falling prices.

- Hedge Against Losses: Can be used to hedge long positions in a portfolio.

- Market Efficiency: Helps to correct overvalued stocks by increasing market liquidity.

Cons:

- Unlimited Losses: Potential losses are theoretically unlimited since prices can rise indefinitely.

- Short Squeeze Risk: If the stock price rises sharply, short sellers may be forced to buy back shares at a higher price, leading to significant losses.

- Regulatory Risks: Subject to complex regulations and potential trading restrictions.

Short Selling vs. Put Options: Key Differences

Short Selling:

- Mechanism: Selling borrowed shares with the intent to repurchase at a lower price.

- Profit/Loss Potential: Limited profit (price can't fall below zero), unlimited risk (price can rise indefinitely).

- Cost: May involve borrowing fees and interest on the borrowed stock.

Put Options:

- Mechanism: Buying a contract that gives the right (but not obligation) to sell a stock at a set price within a specific time frame.

- Profit/Loss Potential: Limited profit (up to the strike price minus premium), limited risk (cost of the premium).

- Cost: Premium paid for the option.

Benefits of Put Options:

- Defined Risk: Maximum loss is limited to the premium paid for the option.

- Leverage: Allows significant control over a large amount of stock with a relatively small investment.

- Flexibility: Can be tailored to specific price points and time frames.

Regulations on Short Selling: Indian vs. Global Markets

A) Indian Markets:

- F&O Segment: Short selling in the Futures & Options (F&O) segment is regulated by the Securities and Exchange Board of India (SEBI).

- Requirements: Must have a margin account. SEBI imposes regulations to prevent excessive speculation and maintain market stability.

- Disclosure: Short positions must be disclosed, and there are restrictions on naked short selling (selling shares without ensuring they can be borrowed).

B) Global Markets:

- Regulations: Vary by country. For instance, in the U.S., the Securities and Exchange Commission (SEC) regulates short selling and requires disclosure of large short positions.

- Naked Short Selling: Generally prohibited to prevent market manipulation.

- Regulatory Bodies: Different countries have their own bodies (e.g., Financial Conduct Authority in the UK, Australian Securities and Investments Commission in Australia).

Key Strategies for Safe and Legal Short Selling

1. Research and Analysis:

- Fundamental Analysis: Analyze financial health and market conditions of the company.

- Technical Analysis: Use chart patterns and technical indicators to time entries and exits.

2. Risk Management:

- Stop-Loss Orders: Set stop-loss orders to limit potential losses if the stock price rises unexpectedly.

- Position Sizing: Avoid putting too much capital at risk on a single trade.

3. Monitoring Regulations:

- Stay Informed: Regularly check for any changes in regulations that may affect short selling practices.

- Compliance: Ensure all trades are compliant with the current regulatory framework to avoid penalties.

4. Hedging:

- Options: Use put options to hedge short positions and limit potential losses.

- Diversification: Diversify your trades to spread risk.

5. Timing:

- Market Conditions: Short sell during bearish market conditions or when a stock shows signs of weakness.

- Earnings Reports: Be cautious around earnings announcements as they can lead to unpredictable price movements.

Examples of Short Selling Success:

- Case Study: A trader shorted a stock based on declining revenue and a weakening industry outlook, bought it back after a significant price drop, and realized a profit.

Examples of Using Put Options:

- Case Study: An investor bought put options on a tech stock that was expected to decline due to competitive pressures. The stock fell as anticipated, and the options became profitable.

By understanding the intricacies of short selling and utilizing these strategies, traders can navigate the complexities of both spot and futures markets effectively while managing risks and adhering to regulations.

Key Takeaways

1. Short Selling Basics: Short selling involves borrowing stocks to sell them at a high price with the intention of buying them back later at a lower price to profit from the decline.

2. Short Selling vs. Put Options: While both strategies aim to profit from a price drop, short selling requires borrowing and selling the asset, whereas put options involve buying a contract that gains value if the stock price falls.

3. Regulatory Framework: In India, short selling in the F&O (Futures and Options) segment is regulated with specific rules to ensure market stability and transparency, which differ from global regulations that vary by country.

4. Pros and Cons: Short selling can offer high rewards if the market falls as anticipated, but it also carries significant risks including potential unlimited losses and increased market volatility.

5. Safe Trading Practices: To short sell legally and minimize losses, traders should thoroughly research, use stop-loss orders, and adhere to regulatory guidelines to manage risk effectively and avoid unnecessary financial exposure.

Conclusion

In the dynamic world of financial markets, short selling offers both an intriguing opportunity and a substantial risk. By betting against a stock's future performance, traders can potentially profit from declining prices, but this strategy requires a thorough understanding of market mechanics and regulations. Unlike put options, which provide the right to sell at a predetermined price, short selling involves borrowing stocks and selling them with the hope of repurchasing at a lower price. While regulations, such as those in India's F&O segment and global markets, aim to ensure fair play and reduce systemic risk, traders must navigate these rules carefully. Success in short selling hinges on a clear strategy, proper risk management, and adherence to legal frameworks. As renowned investor Benjamin Graham said, "The stock market is filled with individuals who know the price of everything, but the value of nothing." To excel in short selling, one must not only understand the price but also the underlying value and regulations, ensuring informed and strategic decisions.

Chapter 18: Continuously Educate Yourself

Introduction

In the fast-paced world of the stock market, staying ahead means more than just making smart trades—it's about continuous learning and adaptation. This chapter will guide you through the importance of keeping up with market trends and regulatory changes, emphasizing how being well-informed can sharpen your trading strategies and boost your success. By actively seeking advice from certified experts and embracing ongoing education, you'll not only stay competitive but also enhance your ability to navigate the ever-evolving financial landscape with confidence.

Mastering Market Movements: The Power of Continuous Education

1. Embrace Market Knowledge

Understanding market developments and regulatory changes is crucial for navigating the stock market effectively. Financial markets are dynamic and influenced by a multitude of factors including economic indicators, geopolitical events, and company-specific news. Being well-informed allows you to make timely decisions and adapt your strategies accordingly.

Key Strategies:

- Follow Market News: Regularly read financial news from reputable sources like Bloomberg, CNBC, and Reuters.

- Subscribe to Financial Reports: Get updates from market analysis reports and economic calendars.

- Join Webinars and Workshops: Participate in events hosted by financial experts to gain new insights.

Benefits:

- Timely Decisions: Stay ahead of market trends and make informed trading choices.

- Risk Management: Better anticipate potential risks and adjust your strategies to mitigate them.

- Opportunity Identification: Spot emerging opportunities before they become apparent to the broader market.

2. Seek Expert Advice

Consulting with registered financial advisors or market experts can provide a valuable perspective on your trading strategies. These professionals are often registered with regulatory authorities, ensuring they adhere to industry standards and offer reliable advice.

Key Strategies:

- Hire a Certified Financial Planner (CFP): Work with advisors who are certified and have a fiduciary duty to act in your best interest.

- Use Brokerage Services: Leverage the research and insights provided by your brokerage firm.

- Participate in Advisory Groups: Engage in discussions with investment clubs or advisory forums.

Benefits:

- Tailored Strategies: Receive advice customized to your financial goals and risk tolerance.

- Expert Insights: Gain access to sophisticated analyses and market predictions.

- Informed Decisions: Make more strategic decisions based on professional guidance.

3. Commit to Ongoing Education

The stock market evolves, and so should your trading strategies. Continuous learning helps you stay current with new trends, tools, and technologies. This adaptability is key to maintaining a competitive edge and optimizing your investment outcomes.

Key Strategies

- Enroll in Courses: Take online courses or attend seminars on advanced trading techniques and market analysis from registered and authorized institutes.

- Read Books and Articles: Explore literature on investing strategies and market psychology.

- Practice with Simulations: Use trading simulators to experiment with new strategies without financial risk.

Benefits:

- Skill Enhancement: Develop a deeper understanding of complex market mechanisms and trading strategies.

- Adaptability: Quickly adjust to market changes and implement new techniques.

- Increased Confidence: Approach trading with greater assurance and expertise.

Summary

By continuously educating yourself, seeking expert advice, and staying informed about market developments, you empower yourself to make better trading decisions and adapt to ever-changing market conditions. This commitment to ongoing learning not only enhances your trading strategies but also positions you for long-term success in the stock market.

Key Takeaways

1. Stay Updated: Regularly follow market news and regulatory changes to keep your trading strategies relevant and effective.

2. Consult Experts: Seek advice from professionals who are registered with stock market regulatory bodies to refine your approach and avoid costly mistakes.

3. Commit to Learning: Embrace continuous education as a crucial part of your trading journey to stay ahead of market trends and techniques.

4. Adapt Strategies: Be flexible and willing to adjust your trading strategies based on new information and evolving market conditions.

5. Leverage Resources: Use reputable sources and educational tools to deepen your understanding and enhance your decision-making in the stock market.

Conclusion

In the ever-evolving world of the stock market, staying ahead demands more than just a keen eye on current trends; it requires a steadfast commitment to continuous learning and adaptation. As the market landscape shifts with new regulations and emerging strategies, educating yourself through reliable sources and expert advice becomes your greatest asset. Remember, "In investing, what is comfortable is rarely profitable." Embrace the journey of constant learning and be prepared to adjust your strategies to stay on top. This chapter underscores that successful trading isn't a destination but a dynamic process of ongoing education and adaptability, ensuring that you are not just reacting to market changes but anticipating and thriving amidst them.

Chapter 19: Evaluate Trading Performance

Introduction

In the world of stock trading, understanding how well you're doing isn't just about watching numbers rise or fall—it's about digging deeper to see what those numbers truly mean. This chapter takes you on a journey through the essential metrics for evaluating your trading performance, such as win/loss ratios and return on investment. We'll explore how these metrics reveal the strengths and weaknesses in your trading strategy and how to use this insight to refine your approach for better results. By learning from past trades and understanding your performance in detail, you can turn every trade into a valuable lesson and continually improve your trading skills.

Mastering the Metrics: How to Evaluate and Boost Your Trading Performance

A) Understanding and Improving Your Trading Performance

Evaluating your trading performance is essential for refining your strategies and achieving consistent success in the stock market. By focusing on key metrics and learning from past trades, you can enhance your decision-making and increase profitability. Let's break down the most important aspects of performance evaluation and offer strategies to make the most of your findings.

1. Key Metrics for Evaluating Trading Performance

   1. Win/Loss Ratio

- Definition: This metric compares the number of winning trades to losing trades.

- Importance: It provides a clear picture of how often your trades are successful versus unsuccessful.

- Example: If you made 10 trades and 6 were profitable, your win/loss ratio is 6:4, or 1.5.

- Strategy: Aim to improve your ratio by analyzing losing trades to understand what went wrong and adjusting your strategy accordingly.

2. Return on Investment (ROI)

- Definition: ROI measures the profitability of your trades relative to the amount invested.

- Importance: It helps you assess how well your capital is being used.

- Example: If you invested $1,000 and made $200 in profit, your ROI is 20%.

- Strategy: Track your ROI for different trades and refine your approach to focus on higher-return opportunities.

3. Average Gain/Loss Per Trade

- Definition: This metric calculates the average profit or loss from each trade.

- Importance: It reveals the effectiveness of your trading strategy in monetary terms.

- Example: If you have 10 trades with a total gain of $500, your average gain per trade is $50.

- Strategy: Use this information to set realistic profit targets and stop-loss limits to improve your trading outcomes.

4. Maximum Drawdown

- Definition: The largest peak-to-trough decline in your portfolio's value.

- Importance: It indicates the risk of your trading strategy and helps manage potential losses.

- Example: If your portfolio peaked at $10,000 and fell to $7,500 before recovering, your maximum drawdown is 25%.

- Strategy: Minimize drawdowns by implementing stop-loss orders and diversifying your trades.

B) Learning from Past Trades

1. Review Trade Logs

- Action: Keep detailed records of every trade, including entry and exit points, reasoning, and outcomes.

- Benefit: Analyzing these logs helps identify patterns and areas for improvement.

2. Analyze Mistakes and Successes

- Action: Assess what went wrong in losing trades and what worked in successful ones.

- Benefit: By understanding these factors, you can adjust your strategies to capitalize on strengths and avoid past mistakes.

3. Adjust Your Strategy Based on Findings

- Action: Modify your trading plan according to the insights gained from performance analysis.

- Benefit: This leads to more informed decision-making and potentially better trading results.

C) Helpful Strategies for Performance Improvement

- Back testing: Test your strategies using historical data to see how they would have performed.

- Set Clear Goals: Define what success looks like for you, such as a target ROI or win/loss ratio, and measure progress toward these goals.

- Continuous Learning: Stay updated on market trends and trading techniques to refine your strategies.

D) Benefits of Evaluating Trading Performance:

- Enhanced Decision-Making: Informed decisions based on performance metrics lead to more effective trading strategies.

- Increased Profitability: By learning from past trades and adjusting your approach, you can boost your overall returns.

- Risk Management: Understanding metrics like maximum drawdown helps in managing risk and protecting your capital.

By focusing on these key metrics and continuously learning from your trading performance, you can sharpen your skills, improve your trading outcomes, and achieve greater success in the stock market.

Key Takeaways

1. Track Your Metrics: Regularly monitor key metrics like win/loss ratios and return on investment (ROI) to gauge your trading success.

2. Analyze Past Trades: Review previous trades to identify patterns, mistakes, and successes that can guide future decisions.

3. Set Clear Goals: Establish specific, measurable trading goals to assess performance and ensure alignment with your overall strategy.

4. Adjust Strategies: Use performance insights to refine and adapt your trading strategies for better results.

5. Learn Continuously: Treat each trade as a learning opportunity to enhance your skills and improve your trading approach over time.

Conclusion

Evaluating trading performance is akin to taking a personal inventory in the world of finance, where every metric tells a story of success and opportunity for growth. By closely examining key indicators such as win/loss ratios and return on investment, traders can gain invaluable insights into their strategies and decisions. This chapter has illustrated that understanding these metrics is not just about measuring past achievements but also about refining future tactics. As Benjamin Franklin wisely said, "By failing to prepare, you are preparing to fail." Thus, a rigorous assessment of trading performance equips traders with the knowledge to pivot and adapt, transforming past experiences into a strategic advantage.

Chapter 20: Build a Comprehensive Trading Plan

Introduction

In the fast-paced world of stock trading, having a well-structured trading plan is like having a reliable map for an adventurous journey. It's your roadmap to consistent success, guiding you through the complexities of the market with clarity and confidence. This chapter will break down the key elements of a powerful trading plan, including how to set clear goals, develop effective strategies, manage risks wisely, and review your progress to stay on track. Whether you're a seasoned trader or just starting, understanding and implementing these components will help you navigate the stock market's twists and turns, making your trading experience more structured, strategic, and ultimately, successful.

Crafting Your Winning Trading Blueprint: A Step-by-Step Guide

Building a comprehensive trading plan is crucial for achieving consistent success in the stock market. This guide will walk you through the essential components of a trading plan, helping you create a structured approach to trading that maximizes your chances of success.

1. Set Clear Goals

- Define Your Objectives: Start by setting specific, measurable, attainable, relevant, and time-bound (SMART) goals. This could range from earning a certain percentage return annually to growing your trading capital by a set amount over a specified period.

- Short-Term vs. Long-Term Goals: Identify both short-term goals (e.g., monthly profit targets) and long-term goals (e.g., building a retirement fund). Short-term goals help maintain motivation and focus, while long-term goals provide overarching direction.

Key Strategies:

- SMART Goals: Use the SMART framework to ensure your goals are realistic and achievable.

- Benchmark Performance: Compare your performance against market benchmarks to gauge success.

Benefits:

- Clarity: Clear goals provide a roadmap for your trading activities.

- Motivation: Achieving short-term goals keeps you motivated toward your long-term objectives.

2. Develop a Robust Strategy

- Identify Trading Style: Choose a trading style that matches your personality and time commitment. Common styles include day trading, swing trading, and long-term investing.

- Technical vs. Fundamental Analysis: Decide whether you will base your trades on technical analysis (chart patterns, indicators) or fundamental analysis (company earnings, economic indicators), or a combination of both.

Key Strategies:

- Back testing: Test your strategy using historical data to ensure its viability.

- Diversification: Avoid putting all your money into a single trade or asset class to mitigate risk.

Benefits:

- Consistency: A well-defined strategy helps maintain consistency in your trading decisions.

- Adaptability: Understanding various strategies allows you to adapt to different market conditions.

3. Implement Effective Risk Management

- Determine Risk Tolerance: Assess how much risk you are willing to take on each trade and overall. This includes setting limits on how much of your capital is at risk.

- Use Stop-Loss Orders: Implement stop-loss orders to automatically exit a trade if it moves against you beyond a certain point.

Key Strategies:

- Position Sizing: Calculate the appropriate position size based on your risk tolerance and the volatility of the asset.

- Risk-Reward Ratio: Aim for trades with a favourable risk-reward ratio, such as 1:2 or better.

Benefits:

- Capital Preservation: Effective risk management helps protect your capital from significant losses.

- Psychological Comfort: Knowing you have measures in place to manage risk reduces trading stress.

4. Regularly Review and Adjust Your Plan

- Track Performance: Keep a trading journal to record your trades, strategies used, and outcomes. Review this regularly to identify patterns and areas for improvement.

- Adjust Goals and Strategies: As you gain experience and the market evolves, adjust your goals and strategies to stay aligned with your objectives.

Key Strategies:

- Weekly or Monthly Reviews: Schedule regular reviews of your trading performance and strategy effectiveness.

- Learn from Mistakes: Analyze unsuccessful trades to understand what went wrong and how to avoid similar mistakes in the future.

Benefits:

- Continuous Improvement: Regular reviews help refine your trading plan and enhance your skills.

- Adaptability: Adjusting your plan ensures it remains relevant to changing market conditions and personal goals.

Summary of Benefits

- Clarity and Focus: Clear goals and a structured plan provide direction and motivation.

- Consistency and Adaptability: A robust strategy ensures consistent decision-making and adaptability to market changes.

- Capital Protection: Effective risk management safeguards your investment capital.

- Continuous Growth: Regular reviews facilitate ongoing improvement and alignment with market conditions.

By following these steps, you will build a comprehensive trading plan that not only enhances your chances of success but also provides a structured approach to navigating the complexities of the stock market.

Key Takeaways

- Set Clear Goals: Define specific, measurable, and achievable trading goals to guide your strategy and track progress effectively.

- Develop a Strategy: Choose a trading strategy that aligns with your goals, whether it's day trading, swing trading, or long-term investing.

- Implement Risk Management: Establish rules for risk management, including stop-loss orders and position sizing, to protect your capital and minimize losses.

- Create a Routine for Review: Regularly review and adjust your trading plan based on performance, market conditions, and evolving goals to stay on track.

- Document Everything: Keep detailed records of all trades, strategies, and outcomes to refine your approach and learn from both successes and mistakes.

Conclusion

In the world of stock trading, a meticulously crafted trading plan is not just a roadmap but a compass guiding you through the turbulent waters of the market. As we've explored in this chapter, crafting a comprehensive trading plan involves setting clear goals, developing robust strategies, managing risks wisely, and consistently reviewing and adjusting your approach. Just as a skilled navigator relies on a detailed chart to steer through uncharted seas, successful traders use their trading plans to make informed decisions and avoid costly missteps. Remember, "Success in trading isn't about avoiding risk but managing it wisely. As Peter Drucker wisely observed, 'The best way to predict the future is to create it.' By crafting a well-thought-out trading plan, you position yourself to shape your financial future with greater confidence and control."

www.ingramcontent.com/pod-product-compliance
Lightning Source LLC
Chambersburg PA
CBHW071510220526
45472CB00003B/974